SPECIAL IDEAS

Falling Into Grace

The Trials and Triumphs of Being a Bahá'í

Second Edition

This edition is lovingly dedicated to

Judy Griffin

She was a tireless travel teacher
a dedicated servant of God,
and my dear friend.

She always knew what I was talking about.

Falling Into Grace © 1999, 2006 Justice St Rain
All rights reserved.
Published by Special Ideas
www.BahaiResources.com
1-800-326-1197

ISBN 978-1-888547-17-7

14 12 10 08 06 1 2 3 4 5

Falling Into Grace

Introduction to 2006 Edition:

When I first wrote Falling Into Grace in 1998, I thought I was writing a book to help new Bahá'ís deal with the difficulties of transitioning into a new spiritual community. After it was published in 1999, I quickly realized from the response I received that it was speaking to the concerns of long-time Bahá'ís as well. Many people, from respected members of institutions to estranged Bahá'ís who had not participated in community life for years, wrote and called to tell me that their faith in Bahá'u'lláh had been deepened by some new perspective they had read. A few readers expressed concern that it was unwise to be honest with new Bahá'ís about possible tests that they may never encounter. Most, however, agreed that to be forewarned was to be forearmed, and many even began giving the book out to serious seekers. My own niece, who had grown up listening to William Sears' Happy Ayyám-i-Há album, decided to join the community after reading it.

Much has happened in the Community, in the secular world, and in my life since I started this project in 1998. On one hand, Ruhi Study Circles, Devotional Meetings and Children's classes have replaced Feasts, Firesides and Deepenings as the three core activities, and Clusters have replaced individual communities as the focal point of our teaching work. On the other hand, the magical New Millennium came and went with no major catastrophe and no entry by troops. In fact, between 1998 and 2005 annual enrollments in the United States dropped by 60%. I can only pray that by the time you are reading this that trend has begun to reverse itself.

In the United States, where I live, we have experienced 9.11, three wars, global economic recession, and a seemingly endless string of natural and man-made disasters that one might think would open people's hearts to a new message. We'll see.

In my own life, I've had two children, moved to the country, and, unfortunately, seriously considered withdrawing from the Bahá'í Faith myself. You see, though I had written a book about the challenge of staying a Bahá'í, I had never actually considered leaving the Faith myself. Though I wept for the disaffected, I never really understood or identified with them. There was always a certain smugness and condescension in my attitude towards them, which God, in His wisdom, gave me the opportunity to examine. My unexpected doubts gave me the opportunity to explore the very foundations of my faith, and anchor my certitude in a place that is unaffected by the rest of the world. *"For the faith of no man can be conditioned by any one except himself."* (Bahá'u'llah, *Gleanings* pg. 143)

I am happy to report that I have come through to the other side and am more firmly committed to the Faith than ever. The experience, however, has blessed me with a deeper understanding of my fellow Bahá'ís who have chosen to distance themselves from the community. I have also had to accept that some people do leave the Faith for reasons other than hurt feelings or drinking drugs and sex.

Obviously, all of the changes since 1998 have given me new perspectives on some of the things I wrote in this book. I have tried to integrate my new thoughts into the original text without disrupting the general flow of ideas. Those who thought the first edition was too honest for a new Bahá'í will probably not appreciate these additions. That's OK. That's what scissors are for. For the rest of you, I hope my new insights will help keep even the old-timers from struggling with the doubts that almost pulled me away from the Faith that I love. I can now say from experience that I turned away; I slipped and fell, and when I finally looked around I was still standing in the radiance of His grace.

Acknowledgements

I won't bore you with a list of all of the friends, enemies, therapists and authors who have influenced my perceptions of the Faith, but I do want to thank those who took an active part in the reading, proofreading and editing of this particular book. My wonderful wife, Karen St Rain; my employees in 1999, Jenna Hatch, Richard Hatch and Amy Eisenhour; my employees in 2006, Brenda Turner and Marcia Williams; my friends Walter Palmer & Rhonda Palmer, and the following reviewers: Nancy Field, Judy Griffin, Sue Hasselhurst and Jan Folkema who gave excellent and detailed feedback. Special thanks to Suzanne Alexander for the great proofreading job. Last, but not least, a million thanks to Lynne Yancy at the National Literature Review Office, who has changed the review process into a source of support and encouragement. She helps renew my faith in the Administrative Order.

The Miracle of Grace

Behold how the manifold grace of God, which is being showered from the clouds of Divine glory, hath, in this day, encompassed the world. For whereas in days past every lover besought and searched after his Beloved, it is the Beloved Himself Who now is calling His lovers and is inviting them to attain His presence. Take heed lest ye forfeit so precious a favor; beware lest ye belittle so remarkable a token of His grace.

Bahá'u'lláh: Gleanings from the Writings of Bahá'u'lláh, *pg. 320*

To live with the constant awareness that you are being loved and blessed by God is to live in a state of grace. But contrary to popular opinion, living in grace does not require us to be especially holy, obedient or successful. Quite the contrary, in order to live in a state of grace we must constantly stumble and fall.

The reason is simple. *Grace* is the *undeserved* love and blessings of God. While we receive God's love and blessings at all times and under all conditions, we spend most of our time fooling ourselves into thinking that we have *earned* them through our own efforts. It is only when we are aware that we are being loved and blessed *before, during and after our constant failures* that we experience the feeling of living in a state of grace. In other words, we must slip and fall in order to feel the hand of God pick us up and carry us to grace.

Grace *is the* undeserved *love and blessings of God.*

Unasked, I have showered upon thee My grace. Unpetitioned, I have fulfilled thy wish. In spite of thy undeserving, I have singled thee out for My richest, My incalculable favors....

Bahá'u'lláh: Gleanings from the Writings of Bahá'u'lláh, *pg. 322*

Each time we fall, we become more aware of God's presence and more grateful for His support. We discover what it means to be *"thankful in adversity."* When we finally come to have faith in God's constant support, then we begin to lose the fear of falling. We walk with more confidence, and actually end up slipping *less* instead of *more.*

When we are not afraid of falling, then we are willing to look up from the path, enjoy the scenery, and observe our fellow travelers as they, too, stumble and fall into God's grace.

Each time we fall, we become more aware of God's presence.

Everywhere we look, we find confirmation that our mistakes will not loosen God's hold on us or lessen the flow of His blessings. Along the way, we discover that it is okay to love ourselves while we are in the midst of falling - that falling is not proof that we are evil, hopeless, or incapable of loving God, it is simply proof that we are human.

The portals of grace are wide open before the face of all men.
Bahá'u'lláh: Gleanings from the Writings of Bahá'u'lláh, *pg. 271*

The act of becoming a Bahá'í is a soul's greatest confirmation of living in a state of grace. God has blessed us with the greatest gift we could possibly imagine. BUT...if our early experiences with Bahá'ís convince us that we must now *earn* our place in the Community - that once we become Bahá'ís we no longer have the luxury of slipping - then we will become even more frightened of falling than ever before. The standards are much higher, and the consequences appear much greater than what we may be used to. These higher expectations can stir up feelings of guilt, anger and resentment that can cause us to reject, ignore or doubt God's freely given blessings. If this happens, then we *will* fall from our state of grace, and it can be a very long fall indeed.

That is why this book is not your traditional introductory listing of your rights and responsibilities as a Bahá'í. Rather, it is all of the things I wish I had known when I became a Bahá'í at the age of 17 in 1974. It is not so much "what to believe" as how to hold on to what you already believe. It is not "what to do" so much as how to forgive yourself and try again when you fail to do what you already know needs to be done.

Since I became a Bahá'í, I have watched over half of the new Bahá'ís I have met stumble over predictable obstacles and lose sight of their love of Bahá'u'lláh. In fact, some statistics suggest that as many as 80% of the people who become Bahá'ís eventually stop being active in the Community.

Higher expectations can stir up feelings of guilt, anger and resentment.

It breaks my heart.

But it also reminds me that if I can see a stumbling block, then I have an obligation to shine a light on it. Of course, the stones that I can see are usually the ones I smashed into along my own path, or saw many friends trip over. Consequently, this book is filled with personal stories, opinions, and occasionally, a short soap box tirade.

I can't promise that everything in this book is "true" in the sense that it reflects a universal experience. But most of it has been true for me. I have been told that some of my observations are more helpful for "old time" Bahá'ís than new Bahá'ís. That is to be expected. It is impossible to write for only one narrow slice of the total Bahá'í experience. If you find that a paragraph or even a whole section does not apply to you, that's okay. Toss it out, or, better yet, set it aside. It might ring truer next year.

If this book helps even one Bahá'í sidestep a crisis in faith and follow the Path with renewed faith and confidence, then it will have been worth the effort.

Part 1: The External Challenges

Understanding the Process of Transformation

These are the earliest days of my life, O my God, which Thou hast linked with Thine own days. Now that Thou hast conferred upon me so great an honor, withhold not from me the things Thou hast ordained for Thy chosen ones.

I am, O my God, but a tiny seed which Thou hast sown in the soil of Thy love, and caused to spring forth by the hand of Thy bounty. This seed craveth, therefore, in its inmost being, for the waters of Thy mercy and the living fountain of Thy grace. Send down upon it, from the heaven of Thy loving-kindness, that which will enable it to flourish beneath Thy shadow and within the borders of Thy court. Thou art He Who watereth the hearts of all that have recognized Thee from Thy plenteous stream and the fountain of Thy living waters.

Praised be God, the Lord of the worlds.

Bahá'u'lláh: Prayers and Meditations, *pp. 177-178*

Becoming a Bahá'í is one of the most wonderful, exciting, uplifting, mystical spiritual experiences of your entire life.

So you are a Bahá'í. Congratulations!

Becoming a Bahá'í is one of the most wonderful, exciting, uplifting, mystical spiritual experiences of your entire life.

Savor it.

Shoghi Effendi says that on the day you recognize Bahá'u'lláh the seed of the spirit starts to grow in your soul.

Doesn't that sound sweet?

Have you ever planted a seed before? Do you remember what you have to do to the dirt *before* you plant a seed? In the old days, they took a stick and poked a hole. Nowadays, they take a big piece of metal and stab and rake and plow right through that dirt before planting the seed.

That's right. In order for you to become a Bahá'í, your nice, smooth, consistent world-*view* must have gotten some holes poked into it. Your previous beliefs have been tested—you could even say you had a crisis of faith. What you thought you knew has been dug up, turned over, aired out, and prepared to receive something new. In one way or another, your soul has been plowed, and now you are ready to receive the seed of the spirit. Thank goodness that is over!

Change—even good change—is difficult.

But is it? Have you ever paid attention to what the seed does to the dirt once it starts to grow? It pushes and pulls; it eats it away with organic acid; it cracks it open with a tap root, and it absorbs every good thing the dirt has to offer. In fact, there is not a single thing in the universe that can change a piece of dirt more than that little seed—because it allows that dirt to be transformed from lifeless mineral to living plant. It is a beautiful change, but from the perspective of the dirt, it is probably a pretty traumatic one.

Accepting Bahá'u'lláh and joining the Bahá'í Community is the most transforming free-will choice you will make in your entire life. It will bring about more wonderful changes in your personal, mental and spiritual life than you ever imagined. But just like the dirt that is being transformed into living tissue, change—even good change—is difficult.

So that's the bad news. Change is difficult—or to use a popular term, change is *stressful.* It's not like you didn't already know that before. You just might not have thought about it in this context. That's why I'm telling you this now. So you can be prepared.

So here is the good news:

1. The change will be for the better (even if it doesn't look that way at the start).

2. You will have all the help you need (some from your new Bahá'í friends, some from the spiritual realm and some from your own new-found capacities).

3. Most people respond to change in fairly predictable stages. By learning about these stages, we can recognize them as we enter them and minimize their negative impact.

Most people respond to change in fairly predictable stages.

So the purpose of the first third of this book is to outline the stages which most people go through in response to major changes in their lives, and to discuss how they might feel as a new Bahá'í.

Then I will discuss some of the qualities of Bahá'í life which, because they will inspire a change in your life, may trigger a stress response. Finally, I will discuss some of the laws and principles that may dismay or confuse you, and offer perspectives and advice on how to learn from them.

When a person becomes a Bahá'í, actually what takes place is that the seed of the spirit starts to grow in the human soul. This seed must be watered by the outpourings of the Holy Spirit. These gifts of the spirit are received through prayer, meditation, study of the Holy Utterances and service to the Cause of God.

...Naturally there will be periods of distress and difficulty, and even severe tests; but if that person turns firmly toward the divine Manifestation, studies carefully His spiritual teachings and receives the blessings of the Holy Spirit, he will find that in reality these tests and difficulties have been the gifts of God to enable him to grow and develop.

From a letter written on behalf of Shoghi Effendi cited in: The Importance of Deepening Our Knowledge and Understanding of the Faith, *selection #158*

Good Change/Bad Change Your Habits Don't Care

One might think that if a change was a good change, and made by choice, that it wouldn't be very stressful, but that's not the case. Most of the time, we think based on assumptions and act based on habit. These habits and assumptions don't magically disappear just because we decide to change our religion. Though the Bahá'í Community has not done research on the stress of joining the Faith, there are two similar life-changes which have been studied quite a bit. One is the act of moving to another country, and the other is getting married. Both of these changes go through stages that can also be related to theories of child development. I will try to interweave all three of these analogies to explain the challenge of becoming a Bahá'í in the hope that you will relate to one or more of them.

Habits and assumptions don't magically disappear just because we decide to change our religion.

Culture Shock

Imagine you are a man, lost in a foreign country, and you see a young woman on a street corner. You walk towards her asking, "Do you speak English?" She lowers her head and turns away, so you move closer and wave your hand, saying, "Excuse me, Miss. Do you speak English?" Suddenly her husband comes flying out of a door beside you, yelling and waving his fists around like he is about to punch you in the nose. You turn and run, thinking, "These people must be crazy!"

"These people must be crazy!"

Now imagine that you are married, and after a month together, your spouse still puts the toilet paper roll on backwards. In your sweetest voice, you say, "Honey, do you think maybe you could remember to put the roll facing forward so it is easier to grab the edge?" S/he looks at you with irritation and says, "In our house, we put it on the other way so the cat couldn't unroll the whole thing." You roll your eyes and throw up your hands thinking, "S/he must be crazy, we don't even own a cat!"

If you think you won't have to adjust to this kind of differences in the Bahá'í Community, just wait until you find yourself in the front row of what you belatedly discover is a six-hour prayer meeting, or you oversleep on the first day of the Fast, or someone tells you that you can't have your ashes scattered over your farm in Vermont because you can't be cremated. Somewhere deep down inside a niggley little voice is going to whisper, "These people must be crazy," and you will know that you have slid right into the second stage of Culture Shock.

The First Stage

The first stage of culture shock is that blissful state before you realize you've been shocked. If you are traveling, it is the time when all the people seem so friendly, the buildings are either quaint or majestic, the food is exotic and/or cheap, and the children are such helpful darlings. In a marriage, it is the honeymoon, when life is perfect and your partner is so sweet and charming and handsome and attentive, and you are on your way to that rosy sunset.

The first stage is a time of absolute openness.

When you become a Bahá'í, it is that magic time when you feel truly blessed by the Holy Spirit, when it seems you have found the answer to all of your questions, and you want to shout from the rooftops that Bahá'u'lláh has come. You want to read everything, know everything, follow every law and say every prayer. You are ready to become perfect—with God's help.

In other words, the first stage is a time of absolute openness. It is like the first year or so of babies' lives, when they make no distinction between themselves and their surroundings. When we encounter something new and wonderful, it is natural to want to absorb it like a sponge. That's okay. It is a wonderful time. It is a euphoric time, but it can't last.

The Second Stage

We can only absorb so much before we hit something that threatens our sense of identity, and then we have to shut down quick.

It is the abrupt shift from blissful oneness to cold, hard separation that is so painful and confusing, and creates the second stage backlash. "Yesterday I felt connected and safe. Today I feel alone and vulnerable. It must be *your* fault."

For the traveler it may come suddenly when he or she feels physically threatened (by people or disease) or it may build slowly as a result of having all cultural reference points become arbitrary (it's like walking on a waterbed.)

In a marriage, the first major fight without a clear resolution may throw both parties into isolation and blame. The sense of being abandoned and betrayed can be overwhelming—even when you are the one walking out the door—because the shift from feeling loved unconditionally to feeling rejected and judged was so sudden.

As a new Bahá'í, there will come a time when you say or do something that someone else doesn't consider "appropriate." Or, vise versa, you may see, hear or read something that doesn't fit your inner vision of what a Bahá'í or the Bahá'í Faith is "supposed" to be. When that happens, it is likely that you will feel a wall of separation drop down between you and the Faith that you have come to love, and you will feel isolated, betrayed, angry or sad.

What I hope is helpful is the knowledge that this process of separation is absolutely necessary.

Whether that wall is experienced as tissue paper or impenetrable steel depends more on you than it does on the event itself. Some people will walk away after a slight misunderstanding, while others will overcome major tests involving addictions, laws and lifestyle issues.

What I hope is helpful is the knowledge that this process of separation is absolutely necessary. Again, it is like the transition a baby goes through as it approaches his or her second birthday. You've heard of the "Terrible Two's" haven't you, and the "NO" phase, and the "MINE" phase? These are a child's way of learning that there is a difference between itself and its mother. A child must develop a separate identity, and to do that the child must physically, mentally and emotionally push away from its original identity as a part of his or her mother. As necessary as it is, this is a terrifying time for a child, who doesn't understand this inner drive to become separate from the parent whom he or she loves. It is only as adults that we can understand that true love requires a sense of identity.

Love of God also requires a mature sense of identity. That is why the Bahá'í Faith is not looking for an army of brain-washed drones. It is a faith that celebrates individual identity, and even confirms its continuation after death. We do not quote the Writings to each other like tape recorders with glazed eyes. In order to truly love the Faith, we must be willing and able to test it. If we can't say "NO!" then our "YES!" doesn't mean anything. Like a loving parent, God can out-wait our "NO's" and still be there when we're ready to say "YES." If we never test it, we never know, and therefore we can never feel safe. (Of course, just because God is patient with us, doesn't mean the other Bahá'ís will be—but that's just one of the tests I will discuss later.)

Love of God requires a mature sense of identity.

When we become Bahá'ís, we jump into the Ocean of God's Bounty, but at some point we have to get thrown back up onto the shore, whether it is by choice or providence. We are asked to *swim* in God's ocean, not *drown* in it. That means we have to study the tide, watch the waves, learn how to swim with the current and keep our heads above water. That takes practice, and that means we have to get out of the water now and then. Some of us naturally know how to pace ourselves; how to choose challenges that don't overwhelm us and how to avoid burn-out. But most of us just jump in, swim till we are exhausted, get thrown back on the shore and then feel like failures. It is a cyclic process, one of action followed by reflection, immersion followed by separation, bonding followed by rejection.

Another analogy is that we are all "instruments" of God's Will. Our heart strings must be tuned properly. But when you tune a piano, you take each string *out* of tune and then slowly tighten it to the point that it is in harmony again. That is the only way to make the fine adjustments needed to sound good. People who insist that they are *always* in tune—always spiritual, always happy, always loving—are usually the ones who are not listening to themselves or anyone around them. They are so afraid of being "out of tune" with the Community that they never learn to truly resonate with the world either.

We are all "instruments" of God's Will. Our heart strings must be tuned properly.

The movement from idealized bonding when everything is perfect, to separation/rejection, is sometimes referred to as "counter-dependence." It is a time in which you define yourself in terms of what you are pushing away from. This can be just as terrifying to an adult caught up in culture shock as it is for a child going through counter-dependence, because there is a great fear that you are about to lose something that you love.

I experienced this the day after I became a Bahá'í. I had a disagreement with my Bahá'í teacher, and was terrified that my opinions would get me "cast out of Eden" so to speak. I had no faith that there was room for "me" within the Community. Happily, I found that there was.

The Third Stage

One of the things that comes after the initial fear or hurt is anger. Anger is what feeds the pushing away process. With it come criticism of the new, and an idealizing of what was left behind. The criticism can express itself in cynical jokes, snide comments, and negative stereotyping. For travelers, this comes out as racist or ethnic slurs. In marriage, couples can start gender-bashing (women are always,... men never...). And in Bahá'í Communities, it manifests itself in resentment for the institutions or judgments concerning the Community.

Idealizing of the familiar can be seen when a traveler begins to talk about how great America is, a newlywed might "go home to mother" or a new Bahá'í might go back to a church. This is a critical time in the process, because if a person doesn't realize that doubts and fears, anger and loneliness, resentment and discouragement are a natural part of any transformation, then he or she may allow guilt or resentment to sabotage a positive resolution. Even when home or church fails to satisfy, such a person will sink into disillusionment and hopelessness rather than return to the Community and try to establish realistic expectations.

As long as this stage is temporary, it is a useful transition period, but if it becomes a habit, it can kill a trip, a marriage or a Community, and it can take years before you know it's dead.

If this crisis is passed, and the traveler returns, the marriage continues or the new Bahá'í rejoins the Community, then a process of reintegration begins. At first it might be accompanied by a sense of surrendering to Fate– "Ah, well, what else can I do?" This can develop into a more lighthearted humor in which one begins to see one's own role in the process. Once you can laugh at yourself, your heart starts to open up, and the real healing/integration can proceed.

The Fourth Stage

The final stage is when this "newness" doesn't feel new anymore. It doesn't feel "different" or "separate." You can't necessarily remember exactly when that "strange" idea, experience or person became an inseparable part of your life, but now they are. What's more, you wouldn't trade them for anything in the world.

For a traveler or Bahá'í pioneer, it is when you know that this new country is your home. For a couple, it is when you know you will stay together no matter what. As a Bahá'í, it is the feeling that your love for Bahá'u'lláh is not just in your heart, it is the energy that keeps your heart beating, and you could not live a moment without it.

The final stage is when this "newness" doesn't feel new anymore.

Now if all of these stages sound like they will take a lifetime to get through - they will and they won't. It is like what Bahá'u'lláh says about the Seven Valleys - they can take a lifetime, or they can be traversed in the "twinkling of an eye." This is because the stages of culture shock form a cycle that repeats on different levels. I like to compare it to a "fractal" process. This term comes from the phenomenon in which lots of little cycles roll together and make big cycles that from a distance look just like the little cycles that created them. For example, a picture of desert sand dunes taken from the sky looks almost exactly like the patterns of sand that the wind blows at your feet. When we become better at recognizing and responding to the small cycles, then the bigger ones don't seem so overwhelming.

As a new Bahá'í, you will be challenged. You will face questions and have doubts, and push yourself away from the Faith for a few seconds, or a few minutes, or a few days. If you forgive yourself for the pushing away, and if you forgive the

Faith for not being exactly what you expected, then you will return to be challenged again. In time these little challenges will add up to a big test, which may push you away for weeks, months or years. That's okay too. It's part of the cycle. Bahá'u'lláh will be here when you come back, and you will feel welcomed again.

I've also realized that this cycle occurs at many levels of activity. My first disappointment was with my Bahá'í teacher, then it was another community member, then a local Assembly, then the National Assembly and even the World Center. Likewise, I've had doubts about everything from a minor quotation to the very existence of God Himself. As long as I continue to read the Writings and live in the Bahá'í Community, I will continue to experience the push of doubt and the pull of love for this Cause.

I believe that the only people who never doubt are those who never think. The only ones who are not tested are the ones who do not act.

Does it ever end? No. I once heard one of the Continental Counsellors say that every now and then he would wake up his wife in the middle of the night in a panic, and ask her to reassure him that there really is a God. I believe that the only people who never doubt are those who never think. The only ones who are not tested are the ones who do not act. Just as the Faith as a whole grows through a repeating cycle of crisis and triumph, each individual must also experience this rhythmic process.

Indeed its history, if read aright, may be said to resolve itself into a series of pulsations, of alternating crises and triumphs, leading it ever nearer to its divinely appointed destiny.

Shoghi Effendi: God Passes By, *Pg. 409*

Mixed Blessings

Lets return to the question of how a good change can be so stressful and take a look at some examples:

the blessings:	the mix:
When you become a Bahá'í you find yourself surrounded by wonderful and diverse new friends.	You now have to learn how to get along with people from social, racial, cultural and economic backgrounds that you have never experienced before.
You now have a clear vision of where the world is going, and you have hope for a better future.	You now feel personally responsible for promoting world peace and racial unity.
You are freed from the mind-deadening influence of alcohol and drugs, and you feel healthier and more focused than before	You are losing contact with the friends you used to go to bars or cocktail parties with. They think you're puritanical.

Please understand that I am not trying to be a pessimist. I absolutely positively believe that the blessing of the blessings is worth every ounce of effort required by its consequences. I just believe that it would be counter-productive to pretend that the consequences are always easy or that prayer and Divine assistance will replace the need for that effort or divert the consequences.

Having outlined the stages of culture shock that most people go through in response to changes in their lives, I would like to discuss the three major areas of change to which a new

Bahá'í finds him or herself adapting. In order to keep this book from looking too negative, I will title these areas "Blessings" rather than "Shocks." But you know what I mean.

These are the external blessings of Community, and the internal blessings of principles and laws.

I will start by discussing the blessing of joining the Bahá'í Community, in part, because it most closely parallels the kind of culture shock one goes through when moving to another country or getting married. These unique blessings include issues involving the Community's *structure* as well as issues concerning the *people* who give that structure life. I will start with the foundational structure. If you have been a Bahá'í a while, this is a section you might want to skim through quickly. If you are new, I hope you will find it helpful.

The Blessings of Community: Structural Aspects

The Blessing of Scale

Perhaps the *biggest* challenge facing a new Bahá'í is adjusting to how *small* the Community is at this point. Not just our own Community, but even the national Community seems to be so small that everyone knows everyone else. No one ever says "Oh, you're a Christian. Do you know my friend from the next state over?" Yet after a few years as a Bahá'í, there is a good chance you (or someone you know) *does* know that active Bahá'í in the next state. In a world where "Bigger is Better" it is hard not to feel marginalized when your family and friends have never heard of the Faith. This can create an undercurrent of defensiveness or embarrassment that can undermine your enthusiasm. Perhaps this letter, written on behalf of Shoghi Effendi will help:

It is true that your group is now still small, but he assures you that your group will before long grow larger and larger day by day. It has been always the case with the growth of every religion. Some pure soul or souls go to some land and sow the seeds of the heavenly teachings in the hearts of few who are most pure and so most receptive. The seeds will germinate and grow in them. The fruits of these seeds appear in the regeneration of the lives of these primary adherents. These primary adherents share the bounties they have received with other souls, who through them obtain new life and light and in turn illumine other people.

The primary adherents are the stars of great magnitude in every land in the firmament of the Kingdom of God. They are the chosen people. They are like candles which, through their sacrificial efforts, are weeping their lives away in order to give light to the world and establish the purpose of their Lord and Saviour, which purpose is the salvation of mankind. His Holiness, Jesus Christ! see how small the group of His disciples was! No matter how few the number of the disciples was, yet they through His power illumined the world. Our Era is similar to that, but through the development of humanity it is greater, and through the evils of the material civilization and negligence of mankind our sacrifices must be greater. Divine light must make itself manifest in our daily life deeds.

"His Holiness, Jesus Christ! see how small the group of His disciples was!"

In the early days of the appearance of our Saviour, virtue was to save ourselves. When we are once established in our faith, then virtue is to save others. The three mottoes of education hold true in our case too. First grow, then become and then contribute. We have developed; we have established ourselves, and now it is time to contribute to others. We have inexhaustible capital. The candles of our spiritual lives constantly weep away their lives in shedding light to the world, but they never become exhausted. For there is connection between our lives and that of Bahá'u'lláh and our beloved 'Abdu'l-Bahá.

Shoghi Effendi: Arohanui: Letters to New Zealand, *pp. 3-4*

If you focus on what you have to contribute, then the size of the Community can actually begin to feel like a blessing. At this point in time, you don't have to be rich or brilliant or talented for your contribution to be precious. It is a wonderful feeling to know that you are needed.

At this point in time, you don't have to be rich or brilliant or talented for your contribution to be precious.

A quick note about our actual size: In a world in which "bigger is better" there are psychological benefits to thinking that the US Bahá'í Community is 150,000 strong. But there are psychological disadvantages too. This number, for example, would suggest that the average state in the US would have 3,000 active Bahá'ís. If you live in one of the 45 states that have less than 1000 active Bahá'ís, you might end up feeling like a failure. If you produce a Bahá'í CD or book and only sell 1000 copies, you might think that people didn't like you.

Understanding that the *active core* of the Community is only 20,000-30,000 people will help you establish more realistic and attainable expectations for yourself and your community. Realistic and attainable expectations are good for your psychological and spiritual health.

So where are the other 120,000 Bahá'ís? Who knows. But maybe if we create loving, tolerant communities where imperfections and doubts are acceptable, they will reappear in our midst. Some of them are reading this book right now and may decide to take a second look at how well the Community loves.

the blessings of space

Along with the size, the other possibly embarrassing aspect of most Communities is the place, or rather the lack of a place for holding services. *"What do you mean you don't have a Church? Are you sure this is a real religion?"* It can be hard to understand and even harder to explain to others why most small communities don't have a regular place to meet. Even larger Communities often have Centers that look more like businesses, schools or private homes than churches. Why is that? My perspective is that it is hard to grow in two directions simultaneously. Our goals for 150 years have been to get a few Bahá'ís in as many places as possible and to strengthen the Bahá'í World Center. That hasn't left much money or manpower to create large, materially rich local Communities.

The number of Communities with Centers has grown in the last few years, however, and it will continue to increase as people like you contribute your time and resources to the Cause. In the US, there is even a new national task force to help communities rent, buy and build centers wisely and economically. In the meantime, appreciate the intimacy of your smaller Community where you can really get to know your fellow believers as "extended family."

Praise be to God! You must be grateful that He has chosen you from among the people of the world, that such glorious bestowal and such endless graces and favors have been specialized for you. You must not look at present accomplishments, for this is but the beginning as it was at the time of Christ. Before long you will see that you will be distinguished among all people.

'Abdu'l-Bahá: Promulgation of Universal Peace, *pp. 386-387*

If you are from a Christian background, you may remember how the early Christians met in the "upper room" to fan the sparks of faith. There is a special feeling knowing that you are in on the beginning of something incredible. There is a sense of belonging that comes from being one of a chosen few. You might as well enjoy it. It is one of the few ego perks you can legitimately take from being a Bahá'í.

Let me explain: You see, the act of *joining* a group usually provides a certain level of ego gratification. It makes you special. Either you are now part of the *majority* which makes you feel *correct and safe*, or you are part of a select *minority* which holds itself up as somehow different from and better than everyone else—making you feel *correct and righteous.* But as a Bahá'í, you are joining a group which is a *minority* and which considers itself the *servant* of everyone else. We don't get to puff out our chests and say "I'm going to heaven and you're not." We only get to say "We are all returning to God. What can I do to *serve* you as you travel along the path?" No "Honk If You're Saved" bumper stickers for us.

It takes a special kind of person to be willing to join the Faith at this time.

It takes a special kind of person to be willing to join the Faith at this time. It is both exalting and humbling. If we keep that balance, we can enjoy the legitimate pleasure of being one of the early ones—people who joined when the Community was like a family. If we do it right, it will continue to feel like a loving family for many generations to come. But the exponential teaching power of being an "early Bahá'í" won't last much longer. *"Soon will all that dwell on earth be enlisted under these banners." (Bahá'u'lláh quoted in GPB pg. 184)* Then there will be a Bahá'í House of Worship in every village and town. Work for that day, but enjoy what you've got—even if it's just your own living room.

Many holy souls in former times longed to witness this century, lamenting night and day, yearning to be upon the earth in this cycle; but our presence and privilege is the beneficent gift of the Lord. In His divine mercy and absolute virtue He has bestowed this upon us, even as Christ declared, "Many are called but few are chosen." Verily, God has chosen you for His love and knowledge; God has chosen you for the worthy service of unifying mankind; God has chosen you for the purpose of investigating reality and promulgating international peace; God has chosen you for the progress and development of humanity, for spreading and proclaiming true education, for the expression of love toward your fellow creatures and the removal of prejudice; God has chosen you to blend together human hearts and give light to the human world. The doors of His generosity are wide, wide open to us; but we must be attentive, alert and mindful, occupied with service to all mankind, appreciating the bestowals of God and ever conforming to His will.

'Abdu'l-Bahá: Promulgation of Universal Peace, *pp. 334-335*

The Blessings of Diversity

To me, the Bahá'í Community is the biggest miracle that God has given us. When I start to get discouraged because we are not teaching and growing the way I think we should, or we have a hard time getting a quorum together, or the Funds are low, I take a look around the room and realize that it is an absolute miracle that we can sit in the same room without trying to kill each other! I'm being absolutely serious. Where else do you find people of different races, ages and economic and educational backgrounds getting together ***without a leader or boss*** to consult as equals about how to solve shared problems? Sure, people can put up with each other's differences if they are being paid enough, or there is a charismatic leader, or they are just socializing or they all think the same way to begin with. So the Bahá'í Community is a miracle. But it is a miracle in *motion.* Motion creates friction, and friction creates stress. Diversity can be the oil that keeps us turning, or the sand that grinds away at our personal rough spots.

nineteen day feast

At no time is the community's many kinds of diversity more apparent than during the devotional, business and social portions of the 19 Day Feast.

Feasts are the Bahá'í equivalent of Sunday morning worship, a town meeting and a pitch-in party all at once. As one retired Continental Counsellor often said: "The Bahá'í Faith is the only religion in which the Prophet made it a law that we get together and party once a month!" With a new month starting every 19 days, that's 19 parties a year!

There are three parts to the 19 Day Feast:

1. Devotions, at which the prayers and Writings of the Báb, Bahá'u'lláh, 'Abdu'l-Bahá, and other sacred writings such as the Bible or Qur'án are read. In the West, the writings of Shoghi Effendi are *not* to be read. Music is also encouraged at this time, both as background for prayer and meditation, and also as hymns sung by individuals, groups or the entire Community. The goal is to create an uplifting celebration in praise of God.

2. The Administrative Portion, at which Community news is shared, and the art of consultation is practiced. The Chairperson of the Assembly usually facilitates consultation, and the Secretary records any decisions or recommendations. This is the time in which to offer ideas and suggestions, or lovingly express concerns. A good chairperson will encourage sharing, listen to concerns, ask for clarification, and take information back to the Local Spiritual Assembly for consultation. But remember, we are all human, so this is also a good time to exercise tact when expressing concern and moderation when offering ideas so that no one feels overwhelmed or pressured by your enthusiasm as a new Bahá'í. Most Communities will

Exercise tact when expressing concern and moderation when offering ideas.

be thrilled that you are jumping into Community life so fully. Also note that this is not the time to bring up subjects of a personal nature. For these, call your Assembly Secretary so that a meeting can be scheduled with the Assembly itself.

3. The Social Portion is exactly what it sounds like. It is the time to relax and have fun, and really get to know the other members of your Community. In addition to refreshments, the social portion can include games, music, activities, movies - anything within the bounds of dignity. Make a point of introducing yourself to as many new people as you can each Feast, and try to arrange other ways to get together.

Now, my feeling is that the most important thing for you to know about Feast as a new Bahá'í is the fact that *no one* knows what a Feast is really supposed to be like. The gathering you will be going to every 19 days is just our current best *guess* of what they are supposed to be. Chances are good that in your Community people have been doing Feasts in the same old (dare I say *boring*?) way for years. Historically, Bahá'ís have tried so hard to keep our Feasts from looking like Church services, that, in my opinion, we threw out some of the good with the bad. Please be patient with us. Share your ideas and enthusiasm, or, better yet, volunteer to host a Feast or serve on the Feast Committee.

My friend Rhonda Palmer offers the following comments:

> The Nineteen Day Feast is the place where the individual soul and the power of the group can come together to uplift the one and spiritualize the other. This can only happen, however, if we go to Feast really prepared for a spiritual experience. It's hard, after working hard all day, to grab a bite, throw the kids in the car and walk into a group of likewise tired people, and expect them to make us feel spiritual. We must somehow find the precious "Ridvan moment" to:

"...free yourselves from all that you have in your heart, free your thoughts and your minds from all else save God, and speak to your heart."

'Abdu'l-Bahá: Bahá'í Meetings, The Nineteen Day Feast *Pg.20*

And once we have arrived our job is not to feel good, but to make others feel good!

"Each one of you must think how to make happy and pleased the other members of your Assembly, and each one must consider all those who are present as better and greater than himself, and each one must consider himself less than the rest. Know their station as high, and think of your own station as low. Should you act and live according to these behests, know verily, of a certainty, that that Feast is the Heavenly Food. That Supper is the "Lord's Supper"! I am the Servant of that Gathering."

Ibid., pp. 20-21

If the Master is personally serving the Friends, they WILL feel happy, whether the Feast is being held in a mud-hut with water only, or in a palace with the most beautiful and innovative of programs.

It is our responsibility to prepare our hearts for Feast.

After listening to Rhonda talk about Feast, I realized that in spite of my years as a Bahá'í, I still had a "church" mindset about Feast. I went expecting something spiritual to be done *to* me, instead of bringing something spiritual *with* me to share with others. I expected the Assembly to fill the role of the clergy and orchestrate a spiritually energizing service that I could come and "plug into." But in this new age, the Holy Spirit does not pour forth from a chalice or a pulpit. It flows outward from hearts that are filled with love. *"Love is the breath of the Holy Spirit in the heart of Man."* ('Abdu'l-Bahá, *Paris Talks* pg. 30*)* If we want to be moved by the Holy Spirit at Feasts, then it is our responsibility to prepare our hearts to love each other before we get there.

The Bahá'í Calendar:

It is impossible to discuss Bahá'í Feast without explaining the Bahá'í Calendar. Now your first question will probably be, *Why do we need a new Calendar?* It is confusing, it involves learning a bunch of new names, it puts Feasts on different nights of the week, it makes my friends think I'm strange...etc. And you would be right - from a Western perspective. But right now, there are at least three *major* calendar systems in use around the world (Gregorian, Chinese and Islamic), and probably dozens, if not hundreds of others used regionally. As a world religion, dedicated to uniting the peoples of the earth, a unified calendar is a basic necessity. Of course, there is also the fact that each major world religion has been associated with a unique calendar, and the Bahá'í Faith simply offers the latest (and most elegant) organization of the year.

Having started with an acknowledgment of the difficulty of learning a new calendar, now let me offer you some reasons why you just might fall in love with it.

Reasons to love the Badí Calendar

There are nineteen months with nineteen days each. Now that is simple and elegant. But each month is named after a quality of God, like Knowledge or Splendor. That's pretty. And each day of the month is named after a quality of God - with the same names and in the same order as the months themselves. That's easy. So now each day of the year has its own name which is a combination of two names of God, like "Loftiness of Honor" or "Beauty of Questions." Each year is also given a special name. Can you imagine years from today, people waking up in the morning to "Perfection of Mercy" rather than the first day of the month of Julius Caesar (July 1st), or perhaps being born in the year of Love rather than the year of the Rat?

Though I have never made the effort to memorize the names of the Baha'i months, I've been told that there is a children's song that makes them easy to learn. Find someone with kids (other than me) and ask them to teach it to you.

Now, if you are quick with math, you may have noticed that we need four more days to make a 365 day year. These are special days called "Intercalary Days" or "Ayyám-i-Há." They are kind of like Christmas, in that they are a time of charity and gift-giving. They start at the end of February.

In addition to Feast days and Ayyám-i-Há, there are also Holy Days. In Christianity, they have celebrations surrounding Christ's birth and death. And if Christians knew the exact day that Jesus began teaching (the day He was baptized and the Dove of God descended to him), then they would celebrate that as well. Bahá'ís do the same thing, celebrating the births, deaths and declarations of *two* messengers, the Báb and Bahá'u'lláh, giving us six Holy Days. But since Bahá'u'lláh's declaration was so important, and took place over several days, we celebrate it two more times during Ridván. Add to these a New Year's celebration (Naw-Rúz) on March 21st, and we have nine days which we set aside from work or school. Even though 'Abdu'l-Bahá was not a Prophet, we still love Him, so we honor the day of His passing, and the Day of the Covenant. On these day, however, we are allowed to work.

So it is a beautiful and logical calendar, (once you get used to it), and it provides many opportunities for celebration. There are two aspects of the calendar that I have saved for last because many people find them the most difficult.

First, the Bahá'í day is like the Moslem and Jewish day. It begins at sunset. This means that the Feast day on April 9th actually begins at sunset on the 8th, and the Community might be gathering late on the evening of the 8th, or any time before sunset on the 9th. Evidently, this way of organizing a day has worked for Jews and Moslems for thousands of years, but for people from a Christian background, it takes some practice. Believe me, I know many long-time Bahá'ís who have arrived at a Feast or Holy Day a full 24 hours late or early. I strongly recommend that you get a good Bahá'í calendar or date book that marks holidays with diagonal blocks that overlap both relevant days rather than the ones that simply circle the day. For your reference, calendars which do put circles or squares around Feasts and Holy Days do so on the *day* of the celebration, ***not*** the *evening* that the occasion starts on.

The other special time of the Bahá'í Calendar is distantly related to Lent in Christianity, but is very similar to the month of Ramadan in Islam. This is the time of fasting. Bahá'ís are asked to not eat and drink food and water after sunrise and before sunset for the 19 days before the celebration of the New Year. Essentially, that means from the dawn of March 2nd until sunset March 20th. Children under the age of 15, people who are old, sick, doing heavy labor or traveling, also women who are pregnant, nursing or having their periods are exempt. Since the Fast comes right before the equinox, we only go without food or water for about 12 hours each day. In the U.S. you can find sunrise and sunset times in your local paper or by simply typing in "sunrise" and the name of your town in a search engine. I recommend cutting back on sugar and caffeine, and eating whole grains for breakfast. The first few days are often the hardest, but I find that my body gets used to fasting fairly quickly.

Some, of course, find this period very difficult, and indeed, a few are unable to follow it at all, but many Bahá'ís feel the Fast is the most spiritual time of their year. I encourage you to give it a try. We are promised great spiritual rewards when we do.

Bahá'í holidays and your family

The first major argument I had with my new wife, (who was a fairly new Bahá'í with three children) was whether we should celebrate Easter or not. To me, bunnies and eggs represented pagan fertility rites (which they do). To her, they were a sweet excuse for a family party (which they are.) So who was right? After many successful years of marriage, my personal opinion is that "right" is what works to promote love, unity and family togetherness.

As Bahá'ís living in an immature, non-Bahá'í culture, we are caught in the middle. Shoghi Effendi says that the Bahá'í Faith has no rituals, and yet dozens of popular books proclaim the importance of family rituals to give children (and adults) a sense of reverence, continuity, and stability.

"Right" is what works to promote love, unity and family togetherness.

Many Bahá'í families have worked hard to create their own Bahá'í holiday traditions, from "Ayyám-i-Há twigs" to Birth of Bahá'u'lláh songs. For some, the opportunity to be completely creative for a family celebration is inspiring and exciting. For others, the lack of direction and pre-packaged ritual is daunting. If you fit into the second group, then feel free to borrow ideas from other Bahá'ís, and even from non-Bahá'í holidays around the world. As long as we don't try to force others into accepting the rituals and traditions *we* adopt, then we are free to do whatever we feel brings our families together.

Three Core Activites:

The Bahá'í Community is an organic entity - constantly evolving, changing and exploring new directions. Nothing illustrates this fact more than the sudden reorientation of the Community around the "Three Core Activities."

Now, when I wrote the first edition of this book in 1999, I did not include a section on the three core activities. Indeed, if you had asked me, or most other Bahá'ís what the three core activities of the community were, we would probably answer with "Feast, Firesides and Deepenings." More administratively-oriented people might answer "Feasts, Assemblies and Conventions" while more personally-oriented people might say "Prayer, Fasting and Service." I don't know anyone who would have guessed that "Study Circles, Devotional Meetings and Children's Classes" would become the focus of such intense activity. In fact, the term "Study Circle," was almost unheard of, while the institutes that they grew out of seemed to be redefined and fine-tuned with every new message from the World Center.

There is a reason why churches have weekly worship, children's classes and study classes. It is that they work.

In retrospect, however, this new focus makes perfect sense. Churches have had weekly worship services, Sunday school and Bible Study classes for centuries. They have proven to be very effective forms of community-building, and they strengthen an individual's spiritual identity. I think that Bahá'ís have resisted these kinds of activities simply because they seemed *too much* like the churches that we were trying to distinguish ourselves from. I actually think that it was important that we took a long break from these activities so that the Bahá'í Community could establish its own unique identity. Now that we are more mature, however, it is important that we not "throw the baby out with the bath water," so to speak. There is a reason why churches have weekly worship, children's classes and study classes. It is that they work. Now it is up to us to find a way to do these same activities in ways that are uniquely Bahá'í.

Now it is up to us to find a way to do these same activities in ways that are uniquely Bahá'í.

Though I am excited about the positive potential of Devotions, Children's Classes and Study Circles, this new focus is forcing the Bahá'í Community to change rapidly. As I've explained before, change—even good change—is stressful. Fault-lines are forming, and fault-finding is on the rise. There are some who are not ready to change, some who are willing to explore new directions, and some who think they know where everyone should already be. These three groups always exist in any community, but during times of rapid change the conflicts between them become more apparent.

I would like to offer some perspectives that might make the adoption of the *new* Core Activities more successful and less stressful to both newcomer and old-timer alike.

First, accept that it would be nice to have *some form* of devotions, children's classes and study groups as a regular part of Bahá'í community life.

Second, acknowledge the fact that in a rapidly evolving community, *no one* knows the *best* way to hold these activities, nor do we have any idea of what *final form* they might take. The whole idea behind the "culture of learning" that the Universal House of Justice is trying to establish is that we must be willing to adjust and adapt our approach to each of these activities. Nothing is carved in stone.

What we do know is that worship, study and service are essential parts of every individual's life. Establishing an environment in which these activities are supported on a community level is one of the great creative challenges facing any spiritual organization. This is what we are exploring with the core activities.

These Core Activities are simply tools. They are not magic wands.

Once we understand this, we also realize that these activities are simply tools. They are not magic wands. They are not "black boxes" that you shove people through and expect magical transformations to take place inside. They are not "one size fits all." They are tools being used to serve a particular purpose in pursuit of one universal goal: "Love and Unity."

Love and Unity is the goal of religion, and it is the purpose of every activity within religion. *Love and Unity* isthe "ends" and core activities are the means. We must not confuse one for the other.

"I need not enlarge at the present moment upon what I have stated in the past..., that the whole machinery of assemblies, of committees and conventions is to be regarded as a means, and not an end in itself; that they will rise or fall according to their capacity to further the interests, to coordinate the activities, to apply the principles, to embody the ideals and execute the purpose of the Bahá'í Faith.... It is surely for those to whose hands so priceless a heritage has been committed to prayerfully watch lest the tool should supersede the Faith itself...."

Shoghi Effendi, The World Order of Baha'u'llah, p. 9

If we approach the core activities with the conscious goal of increasing love and unity in the Community, then the activities will be enjoyable and successful. If our goal is simply to get as many people to participate as possible so that we can put stars on a chart, impress an institution or change the letter associated with our cluster, then we will increase pressure, coercion, and guilt while love and unity evaporate. Of course this principle applies to non-core activities like firesides and Feasts too. There is no magic in the core activities, but there is a magic in the *intention* with which we do them. It is our *intention* that shapes our results. I will discuss this concept further in the section on prayer.

In the mean time, I would like you to think of the core activities in the same spirit as my friend talked about Feast. Instead of asking what you are going to get out of them, think about what you can bring to them that can increase the bonds of love between people. If some of the activities don't appeal to you. That is OK. Feast is mandated by Bahá'u'lláh, and yet only a few Bahá'ís attend every month. The core activities are "works in progress" that the World Center, National Center and Regional Institutes are experimenting with as tools for preparing for future rapid growth in the Community. They were never intended to meet the needs of every individual. If you love them, that's great. If you hate them, it doesn't make you a bad Bahá'í - no matter what some people in your community might suggest.

Devotional Meetings

I love Devotional Meetings. I think they are extremely important in building community unity and in helping us look and feel like a legitimate religion in the eyes of our friends. You see, in the late 1960's and early 1970's there was a huge influx of Bahá'ís who were attracted to the social teachings, but were less comfortable talking about God and prayer. As a result, the Faith has often looked more like a social movement than a religion. We prayed behind closed doors in our homes and at Feasts, but our public meetings and Firesides were almost completely secular in their focus on social teachings. We may have talked about God, but we didn't spend much time in public *connecting* with God. Weekly Devotional Meetings provide the opportunity to bring the Community's focus back to *"that mystical connection between God and man."*

With all of their positive potential, we still have the major challenge of figuring out exactly *what* a weekly Bahá'í devotional meeting should look, feel and sound like. With no preachers, no podiums, no organs, it is a real challenge, and I guarantee you that there will be some serious disagreements in almost every community. Some communities are holding interfaith devotions, while others stick with Bahá'í prayers. Some have printed programs while others do what I did in college and just pass around prayer books and pray. Adding music, children, candles, rose oil, coffee before during or after–these all change the "flavor" of the gathering. And if, for some reason, you don't like what your community is doing at the moment, you can always start your own. The more the better! Just remember–the goal is to create love and unity. Everything else is just window dressing.

Children's Classes

The importance of children's classes is obvious. What is not so obvious is how to organize them when the number and ages of the children can fluctuate wildly from month to month–from zero to more than the adult population of your community. Then there are the questions of what to teach, who should teach, and how. In the U.S. there are people being trained in the Ruhi method of children's classes, but the NSA recommends using the Core Curriculum when those trained teachers are available. This can (and has) lead to confusion

The important thing to keep in mind (again) is that the goal is to help our children learn to love each other, feel connected to the Community, and love God. Everything else is secondary.

To illustrate how we can get lost in the details, let me tell you a story about a friend who tried to volunteer to help teach children's classes while attending a cluster meeting. The trained teacher trainer (and only active children's class teacher in the cluster) was sitting beside him. After twenty minutes of consultation, it was determined that he should contact his Assembly, who would contact the National Education Committee, who would contact the regional training coordinator, who would determine if there was enough interest for a two-weekend long training course, and contact the local teacher trainer to bring him with her to a training center 300 miles away so she (and others) could train him.

He withdrew his offer.

A year later, desperate for teachers, my LSA asked if I would be willing to teach the teacher trainer's child once a week. No training. No curriculum. I said sure.

We had a great time.

Study Circles

I was raised a Lutheran, so I, like Catholics, went through a year's worth of Catechism classes. *Most* churches have some kind of orientation classes, but the Bahá'í Faith, which is completely different from anything that has come before it, has, for many years, appeared to take a "sink or swim" attitude towards new members. When I became a Bahá'í, there was no "Falling Into Grace," no Ruhi courses, no systematic series of classes that I could take to make sure that I had a basic understanding of the Bahá'í teachings. This may or may not be one of the reasons why most of the people who joined the Faith when I did are now gone. For a while, there was a wonderful series of courses called The Comprehensive Deepening Program, but when the person who had developed it died, the program disappeared. In any case, most people would agree that it would be nice if Bahá'ís could have some kind of introductory course for those who want it.

Now jump south a few thousand miles to the mountains of Columbia. They also had an influx of new Bahá'ís several decades ago, but instead of letting them sink, they introduced series of introductory classes developed by the Ruhi Institute.

The House of Justice had been asking all National Communities to develop a systematic series of courses, so when these Ruhi classes were found to be successful in some areas, this information was passed on to the rest of the world.

While they recognized the role Ruhi had played around the world, they also reminded us all that we were to continue developing a culture of learning.

Some understood a culture of learning to mean that we were to learn the material in the Ruhi courses. Some took it to mean we needed to learn better ways to convince people to take all seven classes. But my personal feeling is that we were being invited to learn how to modify a course that was successful in mountain villages so that it would capture the hearts and imaginations of educated and cynical Americans; that we learn how to transform intellectual deepenings into study classes that are havens of love and intimacy; that we learn how to make new Bahá'ís feel like welcome members of our family. That's what I want us to be learning. And Ruhi can help - if it is presented with an open mind, an open heart, and a willingness to listen and learn.

There will, however, always be some for whom Ruhi is not effective. For them (or you) our culture of learning must include other options, whether it be Fundamental Verities, the recently reprinted Comprehensive Deepening Program, or a self-generated, customized exploration of the limitless ocean of God's Word.

The Bahá'í Funds

As you will quickly learn, one of the hot topics at Bahá'í Feasts is the Funds. In churches, they are allowed to have committees of people who keep track of how much you give, and send members to gently coerce you into promising to give more. As Bahá'ís, our contributions are secret, so any plea for money has to be kept general. This means that whether you give dimes or diamonds, you will still have to sit through the call for more sacrifice. The only difference is how you will be *feeling* about yourself (and the Community) while it is happening.

If you are new enough in the Faith to think that the problem is that you and your Community don't have enough money, then please pardon me while I climb on one of my soap boxes...

If you want more money, invest in God.

It really is as simple as that.

I can see that you have some doubts, so let me explain. Remember that children's song by Malvina Reynolds that compares LOVE to a Magic Penny? "Hold on tight and you won't have any, but lend it; spend it; give it a way - you end up having more." How is it that we all smile and nod and say "Yep! Love is just like that that magic penny," when most of us don't believe in magic pennies to begin with?

But what if we did? What would happen if we believed that the money we give away comes back to us? What would happen if we really believed that the money we spent in service to God and humanity would come back to us tenfold? I mean *really* believed it.

Here is a story about the relationship between faith and wealth.

There was once a man who had $1000 he wanted to invest towards his daughter's education. A stranger approached him on the street and showed him a beautiful gold and diamond necklace that he said was worth at least $10,000, but was available for only $1,000. The man was polite, but declined the incredible deal.

That evening, his best friend, a wise and prudent man, showed him a pearl of great price and offered to sell it for the same $1000. This offer he accepted with joy and gratitude. Years later, he sold the pearl for $10,000 and sent his daughter to Earlham College.

The money we give away comes back to us tenfold

The difference between the diamonds and the pearl was not the amount invested, nor the degree of sacrifice, nor the promised return. The difference was the faith the man had in the integrity of the seller.

'Abdu'l-Bahá said that our contributions to the work of the Faith will receive a tenfold reward, and Shoghi Effendi said that our contributions to the Cause were a test of our faith.

> *Be ye assured that in place of these contributions, your agriculture, your industry, and your commerce will be blessed by manifold increases, with goodly gifts and bestowals. He who cometh with one goodly deed will receive a tenfold reward. There is no doubt that the living Lord will abundantly confirm those who expend their wealth in His path.*
>
> *'Abdu'l-Bahá: Bahá'í Prayers , (US Edition) pg. 84*

Many people have expressed either horror or skepticism at the thought of God giving them money in return for money, as though a manifold increase in our agriculture, industry and commerce were a shameful thing. They assume there must be a "catch" to the dea– and there is. It is impossible agree to the deal without first having faith.

Contributions to this fund constitute, in addition, a practical and effective way whereby every believer can test the measure and character of his Faith, and to prove in deeds the intensity of his devotion and attachment to the Cause.

Shoghi Effendi: Directives of the Guardian, page 31

Should we be embarrassed, then, that when we pass a test of faith we receive a tenfold reward? If so, then why are we not embarrassed when our gifts of love are also returned tenfold? The principle is the same. And is not love more valuable than money - and harder to give?

Should we be embarrassed, then, that when we pass a test of faith we receive a tenfold reward?

I personally see money as a symbol of God's abundance. In other words, money (abundance) is one of God's material manifestations of love. But it is not a measure of how much God loves us, but of how much we are willing to receive of God's bounty. It goes back to Bahá'u'lláh's statement *"Love Me that I may love thee. If thou lovest Me not, My love can in no wise reach thee. Know this, O servant." (Arabic Hidden Words, #5)*

So if we all love God, why aren't we all rich? I believe it is because our love of God is selective. When we love God, we are actually loving the names and attributes or qualities of God. For example, when we love justice, God loves us back by giving us the quality of being just. If we don't recognize and love a quality, then God can't give it to us.

So, if we consider money a sign of oppression, or the root of all evil, then even though we may covet abundance, we don't love it as an expression of God, therefore God can't give it to us without it being a test. Our negative attitude towards money acts as a barrier to prevent us from receiving it. And our attitude towards money permeates everything we do. It is like the Cockney accent of Liza Dolittle in "My Fair Lady."

The way she spoke kept her poor. The way we *think* keeps us poor. But she changed, and so can we.

A while back, I read a wonderful story that illustrates our need to change our attitude towards wealth in order to receive it: An angel and God were watching a beggar walking down a dirt road. The angel felt pity for the poor man, and asked God to bless him with wealth. God sighed and said that it was impossible. "Impossible!" cried the angel, "but you are the Lord of Bounty. Surely you could spare just a handful of your riches!"

God sighed again, and said "okay, just watch." With that, He caused a bag of diamonds to drop from the sky in the middle of the road just around the bend from the beggar.

When the beggar saw the sparkling crystals spilled out across the road, he shuffled to the far edge and passed them by, muttering to himself, "It is a good thing I saw that broken glass, or I could have cut my poor old feet."

Though the beggar had spent his whole life begging for wealth, he had not prepared himself to recognize it when it was placed in front of him. He could not imagine himself receiving wealth so he was not open to receiving it.

We must open ourselves up to recognizing and receiving God's blessings .

The story of the pearl tells us that we must first trust God so that we do the thing He asks us to do without fearing poverty. The story of the beggar says we must open ourselves up to recognizing and receiving His blessings (which are often disguised as opportunities or even tests). But what actions can we take in order to demonstrate our trust and prepare ourselves to receive?

We demonstrate our trust through generosity. This also helps us learn to love this attribute of God and to be more receptive to it. We prepare ourselves to receive through service. In simplest terms, wealth is simply the result of producing more goods and services than we consume. If we are not serving humanity, then God can not increase our productivity and multiply our wealth.

So, the more you give away, and the more you serve, the more you have. I believe that this principle applies to both material and spiritual wealth. It is that simple, and that universal.

Our God is the God of Bounty. God can give us the wealth we need to serve Him—but only if we are open to receiving it and are committed to that service. So if the Bahá'í Funds are low on money, that can only mean we are not trusting God enough to demonstrate our faith through generosity, and we are not practicing being receptive to a manifold increase in the fruits of our service.

Bahá'í Lingo

There is no way around it. Every Community has its own language. The fact that it helps people feel like "insiders" does not mean that it is consciously developed to keep others as "outsiders," but it can often work that way. It's unavoidable. As a publisher I talk about "points" and "gutters" and "PMS," and I assure you I don't mean the same thing as the guys in the bowling league. Bahá'ís have their own "inside" language in part because we have borrowed so much from the Persian and Arabic languages; because Shoghi Effendi used incredibly precise words which we have gotten used to using; and because we have institutions and activities which did not exist before Bahá'u'lláh created them.

Add to this the fact that even long-time Bahá'ís can't agree on how to pronounce many of the Persian and Arabic words, and you have a situation which can be stressful, confusing, and *embarrassing* for a new Bahá'í. That's not even counting the times when you are asked to read something for a Holy Day and they hand you a section of *The Dawn Breakers*, complete with 173 proper names, cities and honorary titles. (*Why can't they just name them "bad guy one, bad guy two, head bad guy's assistant, etc.?*)

So let's start with the easy stuff. *Bahá'u'lláh.* How do you pronounce His name? When I asked the review committee if there was an "official" pronunciation key, they offered me: "ba-HA-oo-LAH." But when I was a new Bahá'í, I learned it "ba-há-ol-láh" with a long "o" in the middle the way they used to spell it in the old books. I've also seen it published as "buh-HA-o-LAH," with an "uh" in the beginning. So what is right? The simple fact is that the Arabic sounds in Bahá'u'lláh don't exist in standard English.

Believe it or not, after 23 years as a Bahá'í, it was a Peruvian Bahá'í who was fluent in several languages who gave me the best approximation of how it sounds. He says the two a's are like the two different a's in Aloha, and the 'u' is more like an 'o' but not quite.

This sounds good to me, but does that mean it is *right*? I don't know. How can we know what *right* *is* when our Western ears can't even hear the sounds that we are supposed to be saying? Perhaps we simply have to accept that what is important is not the sound that spills from our lips, but the sound which pours from our hearts. When the experts disagree, do what sounds good to you, and what rests in your heart most easily.

Abhá-Kingdom: Heaven

Alláh'u'Abhá: "God is Most-Glorious" or literally, "Alláh" (God) "u" (of) "Abhá" (superlative of Bahá, or highest glory.) It is an invocation. Like "aloha," it is often used both as a greeting and to say good-bye.

Greatest Name: Any form of Bahá'u'lláh's name, including the above mentioned Alláh'u'Abhá and Ya-Bahá'u'l-Abhá, the latter of which is used mostly as an invocation.

Tablet: A letter from one of the "Central Figures."

Central Figure: The Báb, Bahá'u'lláh, 'Abdu'l-Bahá

The Master: 'Abdu'l-Bahá, which means "The Servant of Bahá".

LSA, RBC, NSA, UHJ: Elected governing bodies - Local Spiritual Assembly, Regional Bahá'í Council, National Spiritual Assembly and the Universal House of Justice.

Pioneering: Moving to a new place (often another country) to help teach the Faith

Pilgrimage: Visiting the Shrines and Holy Places at the Bahá'í World Center & vicinity.

World Center: The spiritual and administrative headquarters of the Faith on Mount Carmel in Haifa, Israel.

Cluster: An area consisting of more than one administrative locality that is organized for teaching purposes.

Unit: A geographic area defined for electing delegates.

Region: In the U.S., one of the four groups of states defined by 'Abdu'l-Bahá in a series of Tablets. Note: the Western region has recently been split into two parts: Northwest and Southwest. These no longer correlate with those of 'Abdu'l-Bahá, but they make the Regional Council's work easier.

Librarian: In most Communities, this is the person who orders books like this one to lend or sell. As the internet makes it easier for individuals to order for themselves, many librarians are shifting their attention to providing lending and reference libraries for their communities. This function is especially important in the area of children's books. If your community doesn't have a children's lending library, I encourage you to start one.

Certitude: State of being certain. Without doubt, confident, filled with faith.

Deepening: Study Class

Study Circle: A particular kind of study class growing out of the institute process and especially the Ruhi program.

Seeker: Someone seeking truth, especially if they are not yet Bahá'í, or are investigating the Faith.

Manifestation: Major Prophet of God like Jesus, Moses or Bahá'u'lláh

Detachment: "letting go of" or not worrying about a situation or problem - leaving it in God's Hands.

Oneness: Just one of those words Bahá'ís really like, but no one else uses. "Unity of mind, feeling or purpose."

The Fund: A Church takes an "offering" and puts it in their "treasury" while we "contribute" to the "Fund."

A New Relationship with Authority

A young couple attended their first Bahá'í meeting in a city in Texas. They loved the Community, they already believed in the principles, they accepted Bahá'u'lláh, but something was still troubling them. They took a friend of mine aside and asked a simple question: What would our role be in this Community?

Perhaps you've asked yourself that same question. Without the pyramid structure of organization that most of us are used to, with the preacher (or boss) at the top and layers of "the chosen" either giving or taking orders, the loose, co-operative organization of the Bahá'í Community can seem chaotic, if not anarchistic! But when a Community is unified, it is flexible enough to utilize the interests and talents of every new believer who joins. However, that means that the individual must look within him or herself to discover what those interests and talents are.

Look within to discover what your interests are.

Of course, you may find lots of people who try to tell you that one aspect of the Faith or another is THE most important, and that you should dedicate yourself to that area (like they have). But the Faith is not that one-dimensional. Look through the writings long enough, and you can find the word "most" in front of many activities, including teaching, race unity, child education, gender equity, memorization of the Hidden Words, attending Feast, and a host of other goals all the way down to learning Esperanto and keeping your clothes clean. All of these principles *are* important, and if we were living in the Golden Age, they would probably all be habits by now. But in order to grow, we must focus on what we can do today and go from there. So I encourage you to look at your

Community. If you are a follower, see what is already being done and ask if you can help with the part that interests you. If you are a self-starter, look to see what needs to be done, and volunteer to become responsible for it. As long as you don't make it your soapbox, you will create a welcomed space for yourself in the Community.

Here are some of the other things which are different about the Bahá'í Community which you might find stressful:

As just mentioned, the fact that there is no individual "in charge" of the Community can be very disorienting. Most of our lives we live in a social format where we either *have* a boss, or we *are* the boss. You may meet Bahá'ís who like to act like authorities, and you may notice yourself wanting to idolize them or consider their ideas more valuable than your own. This attitude can also develop between you and your Bahá'í teacher. When these Bahá'ís turn out to be imperfect humans, it can shake your faith.

Look to see what needs to be done, and volunteer to become responsible for it.

On the other hand, there *is* a structure to the Bahá'í Community, and there *is* a line of authority–it just doesn't revolve around personalities. It revolves around **Institutions**. In a society where we joke that a camel is a horse designed by a committee, it is often difficult for us to take a *group* of people seriously as a source of authority and guidance. It is helpful to remember that the structure of the Community was laid out by Bahá'u'lláh, 'Abdu'l-Bahá and Shoghi Effendi. It is like a perfect instrument which we imperfect people are learning how to use. We must be patient with each other as we grow in our understanding of its proper functioning.

two arms of the administrative order

Put simply, the Bahá'í system is divided into two parts. There are institutions which consist of individuals who act *as individuals* and are acknowledged for their wisdom and insight, but who are given no authority to direct other people's actions. These are called the "Institutions of the Learned," because the people appointed to them are chosen for their wisdom. They include the Continental Board of Counsellors, the Auxiliary Board, and the Assistants to the Auxiliary Board. Since the Assistants work on a local level, you probably already know some of these people without being aware of their position.

Then there are institutions that exist only as a *group* of nine people. The group becomes a single thing, and that thing, called an Assembly (or House of Justice), does have the authority to direct other people's actions (within certain guidelines.) This is the Legislative and Executive arm of the Faith and includes Local Spiritual Assemblies, Regional Councils, National Spiritual Assemblies and the Universal House of Justice. As *individuals*, however, the people in these groups have no authority at all.

The Bahá'í system is just the opposite of what most of us are used to

This is just the opposite of what most of us are used to. Usually committees make recommendations, and the individual at the top makes the final decision. It may take some adjustment to remember that your Auxiliary Board Member or Assistant is there to encourage and inspire you, not tell you what to do. Likewise, the opinion expressed by the Chairperson of your Local Spiritual Assembly has no more importance or weight than your own *unless they are speaking on behalf of the institution.* On the other hand, when your *Assembly* makes a request of you (as an individual or the Community as a whole), you should make every effort to do as they ask.

developing a mature response to authority

Lets face it. Most of us have God, Parents and Authority all squashed together in our hearts and our subconscious minds. Unless our parents did a perfect job when we were experimenting with counter-dependence at the age of two, we have doubts about any God/Parent/Authority figure being able to love us when we disagree with them. When we become Bahá'ís, that love/hate relationship often gets transferred onto the Assembly and/or any symbolic member of the Community. The ironic thing, of course, is that every institution is made up of individuals who have their own issues with God/Parent/Authority.

When a three-year-old says, "I hate you!" to his parents, he desperately needs to hear them say "That's okay, we love you anyway." The power differential between parent and child makes it safe for a parent to honor the child's need for independence. When a new Bahá'í says "I think this teaching plan is really stupid!" he or she may desperately need to hear the Assembly say "Thank you for your input and concern. We will consider your comments and we want you to help us evaluate our progress." Unfortunately, since the members of the Assembly are human and can't always feel the power differential bestowed upon the Institution by God, they often feel threatened, and are more likely to respond with "How dare you!" This can wound the heart and dampen the enthusiasm of a new Bahá'í.

Now, if Assembly members really felt comfortable in the role of Authority, then they could consider the needs of the new Bahá'í rather than protecting themselves. I believe that one of the key measures of the maturity of an Assembly is its ability to respond to criticism with love. The less mature your Assembly is, the more mature you will need to be, and the more prayers you will want to say on its behalf.

A PUBLISHER'S APPROACH TO CRITICISM:

OK, I have a confession to make: I'm a writer and a publisher who can't spell and can't type all that well. I make lots of mistakes.

What that means is that before I prepare to do something, I ask at least three other people to look over what I've done with a magnifying glass and find every single mistake they can. Then I have to look over the sea of red ink *and thank them for every correction they've made!*

What's worse, then I have to send it off to the Review Committee, where they do the whole thing all over again—only this time they look for mistakes in the way I *think* about the thing I love the most—the Bahá'í Faith. When I get those comments back, I have to look over both the suggested and required changes and *thank them* for helping me perfect my efforts at service.

I'm not saying that this is easy. It is hard enough to accept the corrections I *ask* for. I sometimes have to pout awhile before going back to work. I have one customer who sends *unsolicited* corrections for both products and web pages. I curse her under my breath before regaining my serenity and appreciating the service she is providing.

I once attended a workshop in which we practiced remaining calm while a dozen friends hurled the most accurate insults and accusations they could think of. It was one of the most spiritual exercises I've ever experienced. It was very difficult to let the insults wash over me. But my more challenging goal was to let them *sink in* and be *transformed* into insights.

Imagine if our Assemblies took this approach to running our communities... Instead of being hurt or offended when we hint that things aren't quite perfect in our communities, imagine them asking, no, *begging* us to tell them every possible thing they might be doing wrong, and then *thanking us* for helping them serve us better. This does not mean that they would end up agreeing with our suggestions/concerns/complaints. It simply means that they would care more about *getting it right* than *being right.* They would transform *our complaints* into *their insights.*

After all, if an Assembly is *asking* for criticism, then no amount of criticism would be able to undermine its authority. It is only when an Assembly says "we are right and you are wrong" that criticism, *by definition*, undermines the authority of the Assembly and the unity of the community.

"... with reference to your letter in which you asked whether the believer have the right to openly express their criticism of any Assembly action or policy; it is not only their right, but the vital responsibility of every loyal and intelligent member of the Community to offer fully and frankly, but with due respect and consideration to the authority of the Assembly, any suggestion, recommendation or criticism he conscientiously feels he should in order to improve and remedy certain existing condition or trends in his local community, and it is the duty of the assembly also to give careful consideration to any such views submitted to them by any one of the believers. The best occasions chosen for this purpose is the Nineteen Day Feast which, besides this social and spiritual aspects, fulfils various administrative needs and requirements of the Community, chief among them being the need for opinion and constructive criticism and deliberation regarding the state of affairs within the local Bahá'í Community.

"But again it should be stressed that all criticism and discussion of a negative character which may result in undermining the authority of the Assembly as a body should be strictly avoided. For other wise the order of the Cause itself will be endangered, and confusion and discord will rest in the Community.

From a letter written on behalf of Shoghi Effendi to an individual believer, December 13, 1939

Right now, people who are unhappy in the community feel that they should leave rather than publicly voice their complaints. I believe that when, in the future, we are brave enough to hear their complaints, they will feel welcomed enough to return. Together, we can transform our communities into open, honest, loving families in which the thing left to complain about aren't worth leaving over.

the appeal process

So what do you do if your Assembly is not perfect and you don't like something that it asks you to do, or you feel uncomfortable with the way it treats you? First of all, don't just shut down and pull away from the Community, and please, please, *please* don't start complaining to others about the Assembly's actions. The beauty of this four-level, two-arm system is that there is always somewhere to go to resolve difficulties.

What do you do if your Assembly is not perfect and you don't like something that it does?

Start at the first level, which is yourself. Do you not *like* the decision/reaction, or do you really think it was *wrong*? If you think it was wrong, does it really matter? If it is wrong and it really matters, are you sure it was an actual decision/reaction, or are you reacting to an opinion expressed by a *member* of the Assembly? If at this point, you are still concerned, then go to stage two, which is to talk to your Assistant to the Auxiliary Board and/or ask the Local Assembly to reconsider. If you still are not satisfied, you can talk to an Auxiliary Board Member, or appeal the decision to the National Spiritual Assembly. Still upset? You, yes YOU, have the right to talk to a Continental Counsellor and/or appeal a decision to the Universal House of Justice.

I've done it. I've been right a few times, and wrong a few times. But in every case, I have been able to relax in the knowledge that it's okay to have concerns and that the system works. As I go up the ladder of appeal, I know that the power differential between me and the higher institutions will make it easier for them to hear my concerns without feeling threatened. Likewise, I have more faith in the Divine guidance of the higher institutions.

Unfortunately, I've watched too many wonderful Bahá'ís get their feelings hurt by mistakes or misunderstandings and then "stew in their juices" rather than get things resolved. As I said before, the tool is perfect, the people aren't. If we don't use the tool fully, then we can't discover how wonderful it really is, and that, of course is the point of all of this.

My goal is to encourage a new relationship to authority.

My goal in explaining the system is not to have thousands of appeals clogging it up, but rather to encourage a new relationship to authority. The qualities of love, respect, encouragement, trust, openness and compassion that Bahá'ís are supposed to be expressing towards one another also need to be practiced in our relationships with the Institutions of the Faith. For those of us who equate cynicism with sophistication, and distrust of authority with political progressiveness, that can be very difficult and extremely stressful.

Loving and Obeying Even When You Disagree:

We all have a right to our opinions, we are bound to think differently; but a Bahá'í must accept the majority decision of his Assembly, realizing that acceptance and harmony—even if a mistake has been made—are the really important things, and when we serve the Cause properly, in the Bahá'í way, God will right any wrongs done in the end.*

Shoghi Effendi 10/19/1947 – The Compilation of Compilations vol. I, p. 106

The challenge is to love and obey and maintain unity while remaining true to your own vision of what is right.

Much has been said elsewhere about the need to support decisions even when you disagree with them, and the belief that wrong decisions will be made right in the end. But less has been said about the critical importance of freedom of conscience, and the decades that may pass before the wrong is made right.

History tells us that mistakes will be made. Big ones. Painful ones. And it may be a lifetime before they are corrected. The early NSA's failure to support the teaching work of Louis Gregory is one example of this. His posthumous designation as a Hand of the Cause helped rectify that mistake, but it had to have been painful and discouraging to watch at the time. Sometimes individuals can see things that institutions can't. Sometimes it is easier for God to guide one selfless soul than to align the hearts of nine dedicated people who have their own unique visions.

---

*When we place this quotation next to the handful that say, for example, *"To none is given the right to put forth his own opinion or express his particular conviction."* ('Abdu'l-Bahá, The Will and Testament, p. 25) it becomes clear that there is a difference between holding an internal opinion and trying to force one's opinion onto others or the Community as a whole.

The challenge is to love and obey and maintain unity while remaining true to your own vision of what is right—to understand that to *accept* a decision is to accept it as the decision you will obey, but not necessarily accept it in your heart as the right decision. This requires a high level of spiritual maturity. The alternative is to either practice a form of internal brainwashing, or to create a spiritual form of "cognitive dissonance" in which we try to believe two opposing positions at the same time. This will make us crazy and depressed, and will increase the likelihood that we will try to undermine the majority decision.

Rather than fight, complain or loose faith when we see mistakes being made, it is the duty of the inspired individual to *become* a Louis Gregory and find his own obedient path of service. Or, failing that, we must at least try to *recognize and support* those who are walking in Louis Gregory's shoes. They are out there. Even if it is only ½ of 1% of the community, they are out there—inspired and inspiring, open to the Will of God and moving in their own direction, without contending with those who follow the majority's path.

Here's a great quotation about how to deal with your own dissatisfaction with the community. Read it carefully.

You have complained of the unsatisfactory conditions prevailing in the ... Bahá'í Community; the Guardian is well aware of the situation of the Cause there, but is confident that whatever the nature of the obstacles that confront the Faith they will be eventually overcome. You should, under no circumstances, feel discouraged, and allow such difficulties, even though they may have resulted from the misconduct, or the lack of capacity and vision of certain members of the Community, to make you waver in your faith and basic loyalty to the Cause. Surely, the believers, no matter how qualified they may be, whether as teachers or administrators, and however high their intellectual and spiritual merits, should never be looked upon as a standard whereby to evaluate and measure the divine authority and mission of the Faith. It is to the Teachings themselves, and to the lives of the Founders of the Cause that the believers should look for their guidance and inspiration, and only by keeping strictly to such [a] true attitude can they hope to establish their loyalty to Bahá'u'lláh upon an enduring and unassailable basis. You should take heart, therefore, and with unrelaxing vigilance and unremitting effort endeavour to play your full share in the gradual unfoldment of this Divine World Order.

Shoghi Effendi 8/23/1939 – The Compilation of Compilations vol II, p. 10

You will note that Shoghi Effendi's secretary says He is aware of the problems, but does *not* say that He will step in and fix them. He simply says that they will be resolved *eventually* and that our job as individuals is to focus on the Teachings, and not condition our faith on the behavior of individuals or institutions. This requires an incredible level of maturity.

the paradox of maturity

I recently invited my mother to move into the apartment over my office. I am an adult. I have my own life, my own kids and my own approach to the world. In many ways, I believe my experience as a Bahá'í has given me a more mature perspective on life than my mother's. And yet Bahá'u'lláh tells me that, even as an adult, I am to serve my mother. He does not say that she knows better than I do, that she is right or superior. He simply says that to serve her is to serve Him—that serving her is a path to serving Him. Might I find it helpful to approach the institutions of the Faith with this same attitude—to love, serve and obey their requests even when I believe them to be inapplicable to my life as a mature adult? What spiritual benefits might service to parent-like authority bring?

Beware lest ye commit that which would sadden the hearts of your fathers and mothers. Follow ye the path of Truth which indeed is a straight path. Should anyone give you a choice between the opportunity to render a service to Me and a service to them, choose ye to serve them, and let such service be a path leading you to Me.

Bahá'u'lláh – The Compilation of Compilations vol. I, p. 387

Stepping through the Mirror:

As a new Bahá'í, you might think that you will have lots of time to explore this new relationship to authority from the outside looking in. But if you are in a medium-to-small Community (which is most of them) and you are participating enthusiastically at 19 Day Feasts, then you have a good chance of getting elected to the Assembly within the first year of becoming a Bahá'í. If the number of Bahá'ís in your Community fell below nine after the April 21st election, then you may become an instant Assembly member even before the Assembly officially welcomes you into the Community.

If you are not on an Assembly, you could, instead, be placed on a committee within weeks of joining in order to "tap your enthusiasm and make you feel connected."

Both of these experiences can be inspiring and educational. Just make sure that you don't get "tapped *out.*" Yes, service on an institution is a sacred duty, but so is maintaining your personal connection to God. As in all aspects of the Faith, don't let other people tell you where *your* balance between personal inspiration and Community service should lie.

Consultation is nothing less than a new way for humans to think collectively.

As for the tools you will need in order to make the most out of your experience, I could write a book about the power of the Local Spiritual Assembly and the healing power of consultation. Fortunately, several other people already have. *(Ask your Bahá'í Librarian for recent titles.)* Assemblies are nothing less than a new way of ordering the affairs of humanity, and Consultation is nothing less than a new way for humans to think collectively. I encourage you to read as much about these subjects as possible—even if your only contact with Assemblies and Consultation are at Feast.

The Blessing of Community: The People of the Community

Maintaining Your Sense of Self In the Presence of Strong Personalities

So far I've been discussing the blessings of the *structure* of the Bahá'í Community. But what about the Bahá'ís themselves? Joining the Faith really is like getting married. You suddenly have an extended family (spiritual in-laws) that influences your life. You may have joined thinking that all Bahá'í would think and act like the person who taught you the Faith, only to discover that there are some really *strange* people in your Community. *(From your perspective of course.)*

Given a little time to get to know them, you will come to love 90% of your Community.

First, let me assure you that, given a little time to get to know them, you will come to love 90% of your Community. You will learn to understand the Persian accents; you will stop feeling judged by the very rich or resented by the very poor. Black, white, educated, illiterate, pushy, shy, boring—all of these labels will melt away as you begin to see the love of God shining in their eyes. It will take time and effort, but it is inevitable because you are already connected to these people in the world of the spirit. The other 10% of your Community may express attitudes that become the source of your greatest tests *and* the motivation for your greatest growth.

It is some of these "growth inspiring attitudes" that I would like to mention. They are not unique to the Bahá'í Community, nor are the people who happen to express them any less worthy of your love and effort. Nevertheless, they can have a particularly strong impact on you as a *new* Bahá'í, by forcing you to face difficult issues before you feel ready.

One quality, already mentioned, is the desire to be seen as an authority. It is a quality that probably appears in all of us at one time or another. As a new Bahá'í you simply need to stay aware of it, and continue to explore your own understanding of the Writings.

Closely related to this quality is what I call "Old Testament Bahá'í thinking." When a long-time Bahá'í wants to sit you down and run through a list of "Thou Shalt's" and "Thou Shalt Not's," then feel free to get up and run. In my experience, most new Bahá'ís are on such a spiritual high right after they declare that they don't realize how close they are to becoming completely overwhelmed by the magnitude of the experience. Old timers may think that this is the best time to pump you full of rules and regulations, when what you really need is love and patience.

When you are new, you are very vulnerable. You want to do everything right, and it is easy to feel judged when you make a mistake. Remember that Bahá'u'lláh looks to our hearts and our sincerity, not to our detailed knowledge of the laws.

Trying to be perfect is futile.

Even after you've been a Bahá'í for a while, there will almost always be someone around who loves to "quote chapter and verse." They get a sense of power by proving to other people that there is a "right" and "wrong" way to do everything. There are fewer of these people in the Faith, but that doesn't mean they are completely extinct. The ironic thing is that the obsession with doing everything perfectly actually undermines the desire to do anything at all. Trying to be perfect is futile, and a futile effort breeds hopelessness, which destroys faith and the will to try. This theme will be developed more fully in a later chapter. For now, I'd like to tell you a story that illustrates the attitude I am talking about so that you can be aware of it.

Over the course of many years, I happen to have attended two different conferences with two different highly respected speakers who were asked the same question about a prayer of Bahá'u'lláh's called the Tablet of Ahmad. It promises assistance for *"whosoever reciteth this tablet with absolute sincerity."* The question was, "How do you know if you are *absolutely* sincere?"

One speaker stated that if the thought even passed through your mind, then you were obviously distracted and were not praying with enough sincerity. The other speaker, years and miles apart in more ways than one, replied that the very fact that you were concerned about your sincerity meant that you were indeed sincere. If you did not sincerely believe that the prayer was true, then you would certainly not worry about being sincere as you said it.

What a difference in compassion! I certainly can't tell you which one of these speakers was "right." I can only tell you how they affected me. After listening to the first speaker, I would be depressed by my insincerity each time I said the prayer. Sincerity became the "elephant" I couldn't stop thinking about. After the second speaker, however, I was filled with joy and gratitude in the belief that my prayer was, indeed, acceptable before God.

I recently heard a very reasonable theory as to why some Bahá'ís seem to be obsessed with the "letter of the law." It has to do with the stages of transition that this book discusses. Most Western Bahá'ís are from a Christian background. When Christianity broke with its Jewish heritage, it abandoned a focus on law, and focused instead on the spirit of forgiveness. Except for the Ten Commandments, virtually every Jewish law was forgotten. This was a pendulum swing *reaction* against the previous obsession with law. Christians, especially Protestants, insist that *faith* is more important than *actions.*

The Bahá'í Faith, on the other hand, is trying to reestablish a balance in which faith and obedience go hand in hand. It is only natural, then, that in the early years of the Community, some people would allow the pendulum to swing too far back towards a "letter of the law" rigidity. In a sense, these people are swimming in their rejection or "counter dependency" of their Christian heritage. They have defined their Bahá'í identity as "not without law." A self-concept based on a double-negative is bound to be stressful. I don't recommend it.

When you meet Bahá'ís listen especially closely with your heart.

When you meet Bahá'ís and listen to what they say, listen especially closely with your heart. If their words cause your heart to close or the flame of your love for Bahá'u'lláh to burn with less enthusiasm, no matter how logical, sensible or "right" they may be, excuse yourself and simply walk away. If there is a lesson there for you to learn, ask God to teach it to you with love.

culture clashes

Just as some Bahá'ís believe that Bahá'í standards should be the same as fundamentalist Christian standards, there are some Middle Eastern Bahá'ís who confuse Bahá'í standards with Islamic standards. This hits new Bahá'ís with a double-whammy. Many American Bahá'ís subconsciously assume that the Persian believers know more about Bahá'í laws and standards than westerners—especially when it comes to reverence—and yet some of their cultural expectations make absolutely no sense from a western perspective.

A dear friend, for example, proudly described how she walked into a room of youth and slapped each of their feet because the soles of their shoes were facing a picture of 'Abdu'l-Bahá on the wall. This was disrespectful, she said, and no amount of reminding her that it was *just* shoes and *just* a picture would convince her that there might be another way of seeing the situation.

It wasn't until after I asked her if she thought 'Abdu'l-Bahá would have slapped people's feet when He walked into a room that she was able to even consider the possibility that her actions were an over-reaction. At the time, I was absolutely flabbergasted that a sweet Persian mother of two would go around slapping youth in the name of reverence.

Recently, however, I've learned that in the Persian culture, showing someone the bottom of your feet is the greatest insult possible. And because of the Islamic prohibition against images of living creatures, Moslems take photographs (and cartoons) much more seriously than westerners do. Her behavior, then, was not irrational, but simply out of place. These cross-cultural misunderstandings are the equivalent of having a Christian walk into a synagogue and yell at the Jewish men for wearing hats in the house of God! The poor American Bahá'í youth were completely unaware that either shoes or pictures might have any significance at all.

If you are the one getting yelled at, take a deep breath and try not to take it personally.

If you are the one getting yelled at, take a deep breath and try not to take it personally. Likewise, if you are ever tempted to yell at someone else for violating your expectations of reverence, take a deep breath and let it go.

Dealing with Disappointments

You can get everything you need from Bahá'u'lláh. You cannot get everything you want. Nor can you get everything you need *or* want from the Bahá'í Community. Bahá'u'lláh is perfect. The Bahá'í Community is not. You will, therefore, be disappointed on a regular basis. I guarantee it.

In this light, may I make a recommendation? Give away everything you want. It's the only way to get more.

Give away everything you want. It's the only way to get more.

If you find yourself saying, "Why aren't the Bahá'ís more loving?" Then love more. If you think, "No one ever appreciates all the things I do for the Community," then practice gratitude. If you wonder why no one listens to your opinions, listen to theirs. If you wish the Bahá'ís were less judgmental, be more forgiving.

We easily lean towards self-righteousness and paranoia. If we look hard enough, we can all prove that we have suffered an injustice, been snubbed, judged, insulted, ignored, attacked, lied to, wronged. But in proving it, we only highlight in which direction our love and forgiveness should flow even more deeply.

As a new Bahá'í you might look at another community member or Institution and say "But they should have known better!" and they should have. But the best way to teach them is by example.

Far be it from me to imply that forgiveness is easy. It is very difficult, but not nearly as difficult as attacking, proving, resenting, resisting and remembering. It also takes less time and energy. Try it.

The following article presents this concept beautifully. It was originally a guest editorial printed in *Canadian Bahá'í News*:

taking offense

It is deeply disturbing to see the ease with which large numbers of Bahá'ís appear to get "hurt" and at the tendency of other believers to "sympathize" with the one hurt and show their "love" by hardening their hearts against the one who presumably caused the hurt.

'Abdu'l-Bahá asks us not to offend anyone. True!

He also asks us not to take offense! He requires us to regard our enemies (not just our estranged friends in the Faith) as friends. He doesn't simply ask us to treat them as friends even though we know they are enemies. He asks us to see them as friends. Why? Because these hurts are the tests which require us to grow if we are to be steadfast in the Cause. They are the tests which correct the direction of our growth (like pruning shrubs) and test the sincerity of our desire to love all mankind.

'Abdu'l-Bahá asks us not to offend anyone. True!
He also asks us not to take offense!

He requires us to love the people with all their shortcomings. He said, "Do not look at the people for they are full of shortcomings, but love them for the sake of God."

People who are warm and loving are very fortunate. People who are cold and forbidding often hate themselves, are already filled with guilt and fear and only a powerful and genuine love which can thaw their frozen hearts can cure them. What is "love" if it takes sides against them?

A log may appear to be burning but only when the kindling is consumed can you tell if it has "caught." If we only "love" when we are being "loved," we haven't "caught." To know that is to know a bitter truth about ourselves, but it is one worth knowing. It is a very dangerous condition to be in—a completely dependent one. What is the cure? To completely immerse ourselves in the Ocean of the Writings; to pray and beseech God to kindle the fire of love and attraction in our hearts; to take action; to seek reconciliation; to serve the friends no matter what the pain; to teach the Faith and direct the seeker to the source of love and illumination—which is the Revelation. (The friends cannot be this source, for they may or may not have "caught.")

Many people took offense at 'Abdu'l-Bahá Himself. Was the Perfect Exemplar responsible for their being offended? In such a case it is clear that offense can be taken when none was intended nor any cause given. 'Abdu'l-Bahá was the object of the most despicable behavior which men are capable of, yet did He ever assume the role of a man offended? It is possible to exercise the spiritual muscles of forbearance, forgiveness, mercy and to refuse to take offense or be hurt. How do we know? We know because 'Abdu'l-Bahá did it, and if we are tempted to retort, "But I am not an 'Abdu'l-Bahá," the obvious answer is "That is evident, but He is still our example." And the one who "hurt" us is also not an 'Abdu'l-Bahá, but only trying, it is to be hoped, to follow the same example as ourselves.

"Do not look at the people for they are full of shortcomings, but love them for the sake of God."

Bahá'u'lláh says that He desires to see us as one soul in many bodies. The one who hurts us is simply stuck on a different hurdle in the spiritual race. And we, in being hurt, are stuck on another. If we truly believe in the oneness of mankind we must love wisely enough and well enough to pray that we will both learn to take our separate hurdles in our stride, and in the meantime, love, love, and love again.

Prepared by Elizabeth Rochester for Canadian Bahá'í News *August 1969, used by permission*

Love in the Community

Of course, learning through love does not necessarily mean learning without pain. Bahá'u'lláh's oft' quoted line from the Seven Valleys is, *"The steed of this Valley [of Love] is pain; and if there be no pain this journey will never end. (pg. 8)*

I hated that line. It was quoted to me the night after I fell in love with my first Bahá'í girlfriend. Of course, she happened to be the first single female Bahá'í even close to my age I had ever met, but that was irrelevant *(or so I thought)*. In reality, of course, I had become so overwhelmed by the spiritual love of the Bahá'ís that I redefined it as romantic love and went looking for a target.

Those of us from less-than-perfect families are easily overwhelmed by love.

Those of us from less-than-perfect families are easily overwhelmed by love. A little attention, a welcoming smile, feeling special, it is like stepping from a blizzard into a sauna, and we quickly peel away defensive layers in order to soak up the heat. Cult leaders know this, and manipulate followers through a spiritual/romantic/sexual love triangle. The Bahá'í Community is only interested in the spiritual side of this process, but that doesn't mean that individuals within the Community can't get caught up in the confusion. Depending on your background, you may be vulnerable to several side effects of a sudden infusion of love. You may find yourself experiencing one or more of the following phenomenon... or maybe not!

1. Suddenly, you find everyone around you more attractive. You find yourself falling in love on a daily, if not hourly basis, especially with other Bahá'ís. Most of it is spiritual, but sometimes your body wants to get into the act. The person who taught you the Faith seems like the most spiritual, insightful person in the world, and you begin to fantasize about them.

2. Suddenly, everyone around you seems to find *you* more attractive. Strangers start making passes at you, and you are tempted to respond. People who ignored you now notice you. You start to have more confidence, and even begin to realize you are nice looking.

3. It seems your name got thrown into the Bahá'í Singles Pond and you keep getting snagged on every hook out there. Singles from five states are suddenly showing up at Feast to take a look at the new prospect, and you've received two wedding proposals from people you've just met.

4. You try to recreate your family experience within the Bahá'í Community, trying to heal old wounds by assigning various Community members to the roles of parents, siblings, abusers, friends. Memories of family disappointments may resurface.

5. The difference between the way your spouse treats you and the way your Bahá'í Friends treat you begins to create strain on your marriage. Your spouse is jealous, you are more reluctant to go back home.

The fact that love and healing create their own sources of stress may be one reason why we are not as loving as we could be.

6. Your emotions go out of control. Waves of love, waves of joy, waves of sorrow over all of the lost waves of love, waves of joy.... Is this spirituality or psychosis? The act of redefining God as loving friend instead of a judging parent is heavy stuff, and it can feel very intimate. Perhaps you are the kind to dive into this kind of emotional turbulence, and perhaps you are the kind to slam the door on it and walk away. Either reaction is understandable, but neither will help you establish a healthy, *balanced* relationship with the people in the Community.

The potential of the Bahá'í Community as a source of love and healing is enormous. The fact that love and healing create their own sources of stress may be one reason why we are not as loving as we could be. I have seen all of the above responses to the experience of love within the Bahá'í Community. Most of them repeatedly. The responses are completely natural. The question is what people do with them. If the confusion between spiritual attraction and sexual attraction is not understood and resolved, then the blessing of love can become the biggest factor in a person leaving the Faith–due to guilt, anger, pain, confusion, longing, fear or even administrative sanctions.

It is not within the scope of this book to address all the ramifications of the issues of love, sexuality, spirituality and standards within the Bahá'í Community, but perhaps the simple awareness of your increased vulnerability during your first few months as a Bahá'í can help you put your feelings into perspective. Then you can respond intelligently to them rather than reacting instinctually.

Spending time with the community

When and where you meet Bahá'ís can have a great influence on how you react to them. In addition to Feasts, Bahá'ís gather at Holy Days, deepenings, firesides, committee meetings, prayer meetings, unit and national conventions, Summer and Winter schools, Permanent Schools and Institutes and conferences. Actually, as you may have guessed, Bahá'ís will get together at the drop of a hat almost anywhere, anytime.

If you are a new Bahá'í, I encourage you to go to any and every gathering possible. Many of them are even open to your non-Bahá'í family and friends. The smaller your home Community, the more important it is for you to experience a variety of Bahá'í perspectives and environments.

Relaxed activities like schools and conferences are great for making friends, feeling connected and getting to know people's personalities. (Just remember not to confuse spiritual attraction with romantic attraction.) Goal-oriented meetings like the Administrative portion of Feast, committee meetings and conventions will expose you to styles of consultation and inform you of people's character and capacities for service.

Pre-Bahá'í Relationships

At the same time as you are getting an influx of love from God and the Bahá'í Community, you may be hurt to learn that the family and friends who you *thought* loved you and wanted you to be happy suddenly start treating you differently.

You may be hurt if family and friends who you thought *loved you suddenly start treating you differently.*

As Joni Mitchell sang *"Now old friends are acting strange. They shake their heads; they say I've changed...."*

True friendship is based on spiritual connections. Becoming a Bahá'í will always strengthen *true* friendship, because it strengthens our spirits. What most of us have come to *call* friendship, however, is based upon what 'Abdu'l-Bahá calls "accidents of life." We share interests, we have kids the same age, we like the same music/books/movies/sports. We agree on politics. When we become Bahá'ís, *some* (not all) of our interests and activities change. This can be hard for our friends to understand. Some of these relationships may simply fade quietly over time, while others may come to abrupt and painful endings.

The two main reasons why some friendships may end painfully come from opposite directions. The first, which you have probably already encountered, is the "religious pariah" syndrome. If you happen to have any narrow-minded religious friends, then they may never speak to you again, fearing "infection" from your heresy. You probably expected this reaction.

But what about your "open-minded" free-thinking buddies? Why would some of them start avoiding your company? The answer is that when we make decisions to keep our bodies drug and alcohol free, to avoid backbiting, to remain chaste and to turn to God, we are making choices which are healthy. True friends will want to support us in these choices, but people who have built relationships around unhealthy activities will feel threatened.

The process of spiritual transformation can be compared to an alcoholic giving up drinking. One of the first things alcoholics learn in Alcoholics Anonymous is that some of their family and friends subconsciously hope that they fail. That's right. The spouse who pleads with them to stop drinking may be secretly terrified that they will.

People subconsciously realize that if one person can be transformed, then anyone *can be transformed. Even them.*

Why? It is partly because, as I've explained, even good change is stressful. But there is another reason too. People subconsciously realize that if one person can be transformed, then *anyone* can be transformed. Even them. *And they are afraid of being transformed.* If you fail, however, then they have an excuse to not even try.

Though your process of transformation may not be as tangible or dramatic as an alcoholic's, there may still be friends who will not want to see you succeed in becoming a better person. To justify their own unhealthy choices, they may try to coerce or tempt you, they may accuse you of being narrow minded or judgmental, puritanical, or brainwashed. They may laugh at you or ignore you, or they may just stop being your friend. And it will probably hurt.

Though the loss of any friendship is painful, there are some special relationships which can be particularly stressed by the fact that you have become a Bahá'í. It is only natural that lovers, spouses and parents will all feel deeply threatened by your new moral code, your new friendships and activities, and your new relationship with God.

Now I could sit here and lecture you about the importance of the Laws of God, about putting God first and trusting everything to work out for the best in the long run...but the fact is that only you know the nature of your relationships with these people. You have to decide how much your becoming a Bahá'í will change the way you respond to them. What I can do is to simply remind you that *your* becoming a Bahá'í will be the single most important factor in your future relationship with *them.* And on some deep intuitive level, they know that. So they have a *reason* to be afraid, and they have a *right* to be afraid. No matter how smooth and spiritual your process of transformation is, you have, to some degree or another, swept them up in your current. They will be transformed by your transformation, and, as we said in the beginning, even good change is stressful. *Expect* them to go through varying stages of rejection and accommodation.

> Your *becoming a Bahá'í will be the single most important factor in your future relationships with current friends.*

Now that I have frightened you with the difficulties of maintaining old friendships after becoming a Bahá'í, should you keep your mouth shut and pretend that nothing has changed? Quite the contrary. Your *real* friends really will be happy for you, and if your spiritual connection is strong, they might be caught up in your enthusiasm and investigate the

Faith for themselves. On the other hand, if you don't at least *try* to establish a spiritual connection with your other friends now, they may not be around for you to teach later. And don't try to second-guess which of your friends might be secretly spiritual. At least two of my acquaintances decided to investigate the Faith more seriously because I was willing to talk about religion with them even while they were drunk! Even your fundamentalist friends may be more willing to learn about the Faith now (out of concern for your soul) than they will ever be again.

Just try to be realistic. Many of us sincerely thought that if we just sat down with our friends and told them about how great the Bahá'í Faith is, they would *all* want to join right away. It is disappointing to discover that we may only get to plant the seeds while others, months or years later, will reap the harvest. That doesn't mean that it can't happen. In many places, there have been entire families, groups, even whole churches who joined the Faith together. It can only help to try—especially if you try with wisdom and patience.

Section Summary:

We began this book with a discussion of the concept of culture shock as it relates to the process of becoming a Bahá'í. One of the points was that the idealized bonding ends when we begin to feel unsafe or vulnerable. Feeling "stupid" because we don't know the lingo or understand the structure of Bahá'í Community life can quickly shift into a sense of vulnerability, which is why I have discussed some of the unique aspects of the Community.

Of course the fastest way to feel unsafe is to feel unloved, and feeling unloved only really matters if we *want* the unavailable love. That means that the more we love God and the Community, the more it hurts when we run into barriers. This is why the Bahá'í Community is such a mixed blessing. It truly epitomizes the sentiment, "You can't live with it, and you can't live without it." Because we love it, it can hurt us. Just because this is true of everything we love doesn't make it any easier to deal with when we experience it in a Bahá'í context. We keep *thinking* it should be easier now that we are Bahá'í, but that was never part of the contract.

Fortunately, our love for Bahá'u'lláh, and yes, even the Community, compensates for our difficulties most of the time, and makes being a Bahá'í a positive experience overall. The blessings really do outweigh the "mix."

I hope you have found this presentation on the process of becoming a Bahá'í helpful. Part 2 will address the issue of staying a Bahá'í while struggling with a deeper understanding of Bahá'í Laws and principles, overcoming shame and guilt and living a Bahá'í life.

Falling Into Grace Part 2

The Internal Challenges

Struggling with Shame

Bahá'u'lláh brought the world a new set of teachings and a new book of laws. We all know that. That is what we spend most of our time at Bahá'í meetings and firesides talking about.

The Bahá'í Faith also offers each one of us a new, more mature relationship with God. This new, *mature* relationship with our Creator requires us to also develop a new relationship to authority, a new understanding of guilt and shame, and a new level of intimacy with our fellow believers.

One without the other does not work.

The fastest way to chase people out of the Bahá'í Faith is to teach people new laws without teaching them how to have a new relationship with those laws - a relationship based on love, respect, patience, process and growth rather than fear, perfectionism and inflexibility. So, before I share some thoughts on Bahá'í laws and principles, I want to prepare you for a new, wonderful and *mature* relationship with Law.

What Is a Mature Relationship with Law?

When an individual moves from immaturity to maturity, his or her source of motivation (known as a locus of control) moves from the outside to the inside. For example, children (and many teens and adults) are motivated by external rewards and punishments. Money, toys, candy, possessions, peer approval, personal comfort–these are what motivate most people's actions. Children generally struggle to improve themselves in order to make their parents happy rather than because of their own love of virtues.

As we mature, this focus shifts inward. We begin to enjoy virtues for their own sakes. We are attracted to the attributes of God and long to express them no matter what other people think. This is not an overnight change. Some children exhibit this spirituality at a young age, while many adults never achieve it. Nevertheless, we could say that the measure of a person's spiritual maturity can be gauged by the degree to which his or her source of motivation is internalized.

Bahá'u'lláh often writes about the world's need for the external motivators of reward and punishment.

And it was this peerless Source of wisdom that at the beginning of the foundation of the world...proclaimed two words. The first heralded the promise of reward, while the second voiced the ominous warning of punishment. The promise gave rise to hope and the warning begat fear. Thus the basis of world order hath been firmly established upon these twin principles.

Bahá'u'lláh: *Tablets of Bahá'u'lláh*, pg. 66

In the conduct of life, man is actuated by two main motives: 'The Hope for Reward' and 'The Fear of Punishment.'

'Abdu'l-Bahá: Paris Talks, *pg. 157*

While proclaiming the need for reward and punishment, the Writings also express the hope that people will mature beyond the external manifestation of them. The Báb said:

"That which is worthy of His Essence is to worship Him for His sake, without fear of fire, or hope of paradise.

The Báb: *Selections from the Writings of the Báb*, pg. 78

If we associate "worship" of God with love of His attributes, then we can think of our love of virtue as the internalization of the principle of reward. In other words, we recognize the attainment of Godly virtues as its own reward. Paradise *is* the spiritual growth that comes through obedience. There is no separation between obedience and reward because the virtue demonstrated by obedience is itself the reward.

So what do we call the internalization of the principle of punishment?

Bahá'u'lláh calls it shame.

Verily I say: The fear of God hath ever been a sure defence and a safe stronghold for all the peoples of the world. It is the chief cause of the protection of mankind, and the supreme instrument for its preservation. Indeed, there existeth in man a faculty which deterreth him from, and guardeth him against, whatever is unworthy and unseemly, and which is known as his sense of shame. This, however, is confined to but a few; all have not possessed, and do not possess, it.

Bahá'u'lláh: Epistle to the Son of the Wolf, *pg. 27*

The communities must punish the oppressor, the murderer, the malefactor, so as to warn and restrain others from committing like crimes. But the most essential thing is that the people must be educated in such a way that no crimes will be committed; for it is possible to educate the masses so effectively that they will avoid and shrink from perpetrating crimes, so that the crime itself will appear to them as the greatest chastisement, the utmost condemnation and torment. Therefore, no crimes which require punishment will be committed.

'Abdu'l-Bahá: Some Answered Questions, *pp. 268-269*

Shame is an internalization of the fear of God.

Shame is an internalization of the fear of God. It makes us feel bad, therefore it is a self-inflicted punishment.

You will note that Bahá'u'lláh suggests that very few people have the faculty of shame, while 'Abdu'l-Bahá states that it is possible to educate the masses so that it becomes the primary deterrent to disobedience. I have come to believe that the difference between these two perspectives is an indication of the transitional times we are living in. Just as an individual's capacity to feel shame increases as his or her source of motivation shifts inward with maturity, so does humanity's collective capacity for shame increase as society matures.

What this means on a practical, psychological and social level is that our culture is trying to impose a reward and punishment model for motivation on some people who are already overwhelmed by shame. At the same time, we try to shame other people into obedience when they only respond to external rewards and punishments.

We often compare current social chaos to the stage of adolescence. If we consider that at least some of the difficulties of adolescence come from the shift from external to internal sources of motivation, then we can see why attitudes towards reward and punishment, love and shame have shaken the foundations of today's personal, social and religious institutions. Shame has a subtle but powerful impact on so many areas of our lives–including the rise of New-Age religions, drug abuse, crime, fundamentalism and immorality that I will have to save much of what I would like to say for a future book. For now I will limit my comments to the effect of shame on the Bahá'í Community.

Shame in the Bahá'í Community

It would be reasonable to assume that anyone who was willing to look into a new religion in spite of the disdain of his or her friends, family and neighbors would have to be more internally motivated than the average person. This suggests that most Bahá'ís start out with a more developed sense of shame than other people do. Nevertheless, we come from a Judeo-Christian culture that is strongly organized around a reward and punishment model. This puts us, essentially, in two worlds at once–expecting, and sometimes even creating a double dose of punishment for each of our mistakes. Unless we quickly come to a healthy understanding of shame, we run the risk of being overwhelmed and swept away from the rewarding side of the Faith.

how shame works

First of all, we need to know what healthy shame is. Shame is simply an emotional reaction to a flash of self-awareness in which we realize that we are not perfect—that we are, in fact, human. This is a good thing. Being human is a good thing. Knowing we are human is a good thing. Knowing that we are not perfect is a very good thing. Shame is like a little alarm that buzzes when we make a mistake. It lets us know that we need to adjust our behavior. Without it, we cannot recognize or learn from mistakes. We cannot become better.

Shame is simply an emotional reaction to a flash of self-awareness in which we realize that we are not perfect.

So healthy shame is a good thing. So how does it become unhealthy? By combining it with two unhealthy attitudes that are holdovers from a less mature world view. The first is perfectionism. The second is black and white thinking (also known as "all or nothing" thinking).

When we do anything, we are really making a choice between what we did and what we did not do. These choices are rarely earth-shattering, and they usually do not involve Bahá'í law. They simply involve an attempt to balance competing goals. When added together over the course of our lives, however, these choices define who we are and create our legacy. The twinge of shame simply tells us that the decision we just made could have been better. This is a good thing because it allows us to either change our decision or make a different one in the future.

Our "shame meter" is designed to sound only if the difference between our two choices is moderately significant. Like a smoke detector, it is designed to ignore household dust or even Chinese stir-fry cooking. It only sounds if we are in spiritual danger. If, however, we are perfectionists, then our internal alarm is set for zero tolerance. Since perfection is impossible, our shame response gets stuck in the ON position permanently.

If we are perfectionists, then our internal shame alarm is set for zero tolerance.

Likewise, black and white thinking—the belief that everything is either right or wrong, good or bad, saved or damned—locks our shame meters on full alert. It doesn't matter whether we pretend that we are godly or unrepentant, there is always a part of us that knows that we aren't 100% right, so we secretly feel we must be 100% wrong. As Bahá'ís from a Western background, we are raised with a belief in original sin and carry a saved/damned duality deep in our psyches. As a friend said about her days as a Christian: "I went back and got 'saved' several times because it never felt like it really 'took.'" *Knowing* we are forgiven and *feeling* forgiven are two very different things. When we feel *unforgivable* we continue to punish ourselves with shame.

We all know what people do with smoke detectors that have zero tolerance. If it goes off every time we cook a meal, light a candle, or smoke a cigarette, then pretty soon we decide to unplug the battery. No one can live with a smoke alarm going off in his head every minute. Likewise, no one can be happy when tormented by shame. We have to find a way to escape the buzzing alarm, the flush of embarrassment, the pang of guilt and the wave of regret, that we experience when shame comes to dominate our lives.

Given the fact that perfectionism and black/white thinking have dominated Western culture for thousands of years, it is understandable that many people have chosen to *react* to these influences by swinging 180^0 in the opposite direction. Rather than *fixing* the "shame alarm" by developing reasonable personal expectations and learning to appreciate the full spectrum of moral choices, we have tried to simply pull the plug on shame. When faced with our inability to be perfect Bahá'ís, many of us simply leave.

Those of us who do not leave develop other "coping skills" to help us deal with our perceived failures. For example, we may put on masks, isolate ourselves or blame the Assembly. We may become "Guardians of Righteousness" and distract ourselves from our faults by focusing on others'. We may decide that everything is "the Will of God" so the consequences of our actions are not our fault, or decide that we simply don't matter–that God doesn't care if we are good Bahá'ís or not because we aren't worthy of His attention. Some of us become more and more blatantly disobedient in hopes of either getting kicked out of the Faith (so that we don't have to take responsibility for quitting) or being punished by God (which proves that He has finally noticed us).

shame spirals

As Bahá'ís, we do not have the luxury of responding to shame the way other people do. They short-circuit their black and white thinking by proclaiming that there is no such thing as right and wrong. They escape their struggle for perfection by abandoning the struggle for any progress at all. Since shame is the direct consequence of choice, many abandon their sense of responsibility by choosing to do nothing but distract themselves with meaningless entertainment. But as Bahá'ís, we know that there is a spiritual path to follow, and that our efforts along that path will make a difference to our own souls and to the world around us. When faced with an entire book of laws, we are torn between our

Bahá'ís cannot responding to shame by proclaiming that there is no such thing as right and wrong.

desire to follow our friends into amoral self-indulgence and our attraction to a standard that we feel incapable of even approaching.

Since we cannot permanently "pull the plug" on shame like many of our friends, Bahá'ís are particularly susceptible to the temptation of short-term fixes. Drugs, alcohol, sex, pornography, over-eating, shopping, gambling, television, web-surfing, games, gossip, sleep, and even work can be used to temporarily numb or distract us from our feelings of shame. An over-eater feels great for the 20 minutes it takes to eat a pint of ice cream, and the TV-addict is dead to shame as long as the tube is on. The problem for Bahá'ís is that when we stop our numbing behavior, our strong sense of Bahá'í responsibility kicks in and we feel even more gluttonous, lazy, evil or sick than we did before. When this happens, it is even more tempting to do it again. This is what is called a shame spiral. The very behavior that numbs the shame also feeds the shame. Bahá'í law prohibits some of these numbing behaviors, but many "legal" behaviors are just as effective at both numbing and shaming. People who are caught in this spiral are miserable, but are too ashamed to ask for help. Unfortunately, they make up a larger percentage of the Bahá'í Community that we are willing to admit.

Shame Spirals can only be transformed through love, understanding, forgiveness and intimacy.

"Shame Spirals" and the many other "coping skills" mentioned earlier are the result of hyperactive shame. They will not be solved by increasing the shame and fear through threats or finger shaking. They will not be changed through a "more thorough knowledge of the laws." They can only be transformed through love, understanding, forgiveness and intimacy.

alternatives to perfectionism

For us to develop healthy shame, we must silence the constant background noise and return shame to its proper role as a warning system. To do this, we must outgrow the black/white perfectionist thinking that we learned when we were children. A mature individual is able to recognize options as better and worse, rather than as good and bad. An adult should be able to see the consequences of their choices as reasonable successes or relative failures, rather than wins and losses. This is the Bahá'í perspective.

The foundation of Progressive Revelation is the concept that truth is relative, that growth is a process with no end-point.

The foundation of Progressive Revelation is the concept that truth is relative, that growth is a process with no end-point, that right and wrong, good and evil are not opposites, but relative positions on a continuum. This perspective is radically different from that of our Christian culture, and it is critical to an understanding of the Bahá'í World Order. If we do not learn to apply these spiritual principles to our understanding of Bahá'í laws and standards, then we are dissociating the spiritual and administrative principles of the Faith. This can cause the Community (or at least our relationship to it) to disintegrate.

To dissociate the administrative principles of the Cause from the purely spiritual and humanitarian teachings would be tantamount to a mutilation of the body of the Cause, a separation that can only result in the disintegration of its component parts, and the extinction of the Faith itself.

Shoghi Effendi: The World Order of Bahá'u'lláh, *pg. 5*

Here is what 'Abdu'l-Bahá says about perfection, good and evil, the relativity of virtues, and the process of growth towards God. I encourage you to study these quotations in order to internalize the ideas that will help you re-calibrate your "shame meter." Understanding that God neither expects nor desires perfection can help you accept your mistakes as learning experiences. Recognizing that some of your most "shameful" qualities can be seen as virtues in the rough may allow you to love and forgive those aspects of yourself that you try hardest to hide. Once you have gained *understanding*, then you can move on to *forgiveness* and even *intimacy*.

"In creation there is no evil; all is good."

> *In creation there is no evil; all is good. Certain qualities and natures innate in some men and apparently blameworthy are not so in reality. For example, from the beginning of his life you can see in a nursing child the signs of greed, of anger and of temper. Then, it may be said, good and evil are innate in the reality of man, and this is contrary to the pure goodness of nature and creation. The answer to this is that greed, which is to ask for something more, is a praiseworthy quality provided that it is used suitably. So if a man is greedy to acquire science and knowledge, or to become compassionate, generous and just, it is most praiseworthy. If he exercises his anger and wrath against the bloodthirsty tyrants who are like ferocious beasts, it is very praiseworthy; but if he does not use these qualities in a right way, they are blameworthy.*
>
> *Then it is evident that in creation and nature evil does not exist at all; but when the natural qualities of man are used in an unlawful way, they are blameworthy. So if a rich and generous person gives a sum of money to a poor man for his own necessities, and if the poor man spends that sum of money on unlawful things, that will be blameworthy. It is the same with all the natural qualities of man, which constitute the capital of life; if they be used and displayed in an unlawful way, they become blameworthy. Therefore, it is clear that creation is purely good. Consider that the worst of*

qualities and most odious of attributes, which is the foundation of all evil, is lying. No worse or more blameworthy quality than this can be imagined to exist; it is the destroyer of all human perfections and the cause of innumerable vices. There is no worse characteristic than this; it is the foundation of all evils. Notwithstanding all this, if a doctor consoles a sick man by saying, "Thank God you are better, and there is hope of your recovery," though these words are contrary to the truth, yet they may become the consolation of the patient and the turning point of the illness. This is not blameworthy.

'Abdu'l-Bahá: Some Answered Questions, *pp. 215-216*

Briefly, the intellectual realities, such as all the qualities and admirable perfections of man, are purely good, and exist. Evil is simply their nonexistence. So ignorance is the want of knowledge; error is the want of guidance; forgetfulness is the want of memory; stupidity is the want of good sense. All these things have no real existence.

In the same way, the sensible realities are absolutely good, and evil is due to their nonexistence – that is to say, blindness is the want of sight, deafness is the want of hearing, poverty is the want of wealth, illness is the want of health, death is the want of life, and weakness is the want of strength.

Nevertheless a doubt occurs to the mind – that is, scorpions and serpents are poisonous. Are they good or evil, for they are existing beings? Yes, a scorpion is evil in relation to man; a serpent is evil in relation to man; but in relation to themselves they are not evil, for their poison is their weapon, and by their sting they defend themselves. But as the elements of their poison do not agree with our elements – that is to say, as there is antagonism between these different elements, therefore, this antagonism is evil; but in reality as regards themselves they are good.

"...it is possible that one thing in relation to another may be evil, and at the same time within the limits of its proper being it may not be evil....."

The epitome of this discourse is that it is possible that one thing in relation to another may be evil, and at the same time within the limits of its proper being it may not be evil. Then it is proved that there is no evil in existence; all that God created He created good.

This evil is nothingness; so death is the absence of life. When man no longer receives life, he dies. Darkness is the absence of light: when there is no light, there is darkness. Light is an existing thing, but darkness is nonexistent. Wealth is an existing thing, but poverty is nonexisting.

Then it is evident that all evils return to nonexistence. Good exists; evil is nonexistent.

'Abdu'l-Bahá: Some Answered Questions, *pp. 263-264*

You may have noticed that there is a big difference between the Bahá'í concept of good and evil and both the Christian and the New Age perspectives. Christians see good and evil as opposing forces. This leaves individuals feeling trapped in an internal battle. Things are black or white. There is no middle ground, no shades of gray, so every slip from perfection is a fall into hell. The New Age movement generally dismisses distinctions entirely. Instead of acknowledging the gray area between light and darkness, they ignore darkness entirely, claiming that all actions are equally good because we are the creators of our own reality.

The Bahá'í view is that good and bad, light and dark, are only meaningful when considered in relation to one another.

The Bahá'í view is that good and bad, light and dark, are only meaningful when considered in relation to one another. Life is a process of moving from darker grays to lighter grays. Where we stand is not as important as which direction we are moving in. We are not simply "wise." We are either *more* or *less* "wise" than we were yesterday. We should not feel shame for being imperfect. We should only be alarmed if we do something that moves us *backwards* dramatically.

In the same way the growth and development of all beings is gradual; this is the universal divine organization and the natural system. The seed does not at once become a tree; the embryo does not at once become a man; the mineral does not suddenly become a stone. No, they grow and develop gradually and attain the limit of perfection.

All beings, whether large or small, were created perfect and complete from the first, but their perfections appear in them by degrees. The organization of God is one; the evolution of existence is one; the divine system is one. Whether they be small or great beings, all are subject to one law and system. Each seed has in it from the first all the vegetable perfections. For example, in the seed all the vegetable perfections exist from the beginning, but not visibly; afterward little by little they appear. So it is first the shoot which appears from the seed, then the branches, leaves, blossoms and fruits; but from the beginning of its existence all these things are in the seed, potentially, though not apparently.

"All beings, whether large or small, were created perfect and complete from the first, but their perfections appear in them by degrees."

In the same way, the embryo possesses from the first all perfections, such as the spirit, the mind, the sight, the smell, the taste – in one word, all the powers – but they are not visible and become so only by degrees.

Similarly, the terrestrial globe from the beginning was created with all its elements, substances, minerals, atoms and organisms; but these only appeared by degrees: first the mineral, then the plant, afterward the animal, and finally man. But from the first these kinds and species existed, but were undeveloped in the terrestrial globe, and then appeared only gradually. For the supreme organization of God, and the universal natural system, surround all beings, and all are subject to this rule. When you consider this universal system, you see that there is not one of the beings which at its coming into existence has reached the limit of perfection. No, they gradually grow and develop, and then attain the degree of perfection.

'Abdu'l-Bahá: Some Answered Questions, *pp. 198-199*

For example, you cannot see a ruby in the mineral kingdom, a rose in the vegetable kingdom, or a nightingale in the animal kingdom, without imagining that there might be better specimens. As the divine bounties are endless, so human perfections are endless. If it were possible to reach a limit of perfection, then one of the realities of the beings might reach the condition of being independent of God, and the contingent might attain to the condition of the absolute. But for every being there is a point which it cannot overpass – that is to say, he who is in the condition of servitude, however far he may progress in gaining limitless perfections, will never reach the condition of Deity.

'Abdu'l-Bahá: Some Answered Questions, *pg. 230*

The reason of the mission of the Prophets is to educate men, so that this piece of coal may become a diamond, and this fruitless tree may be engrafted and yield the sweetest, most delicious fruits. When man reaches the noblest state in the world of humanity, then he can make further progress in the conditions of perfection, but not in state; for such states are limited, but the divine perfections are endless.

Both before and after putting off this material form, there is progress in perfection but not in state. So beings are consummated in perfect man. There is no other being higher than a perfect man. But man when he has reached this state can still make progress in perfections but not in state because there is no state higher than that of a perfect man to which he can transfer himself. He only progresses in the state of humanity, for the human perfections are infinite. Thus, however learned a man may be, we can imagine one more learned.

Hence, as the perfections of humanity are endless, man can also make progress in perfections after leaving this world.

'Abdu'l-Bahá: Some Answered Questions, *pp. 236-237*

Know that nothing which exists remains in a state of repose – that is to say, all things are in motion. Everything is either growing or declining; all things are either coming from nonexistence into being, or going from existence into nonexistence. So this flower, this hyacinth, during a certain period of time was coming from the world of nonexistence into being, and now it is going from being into nonexistence. This state of motion is said to be essential – that is, natural; it cannot be separated from beings because it is their essential requirement, as it is the essential requirement of fire to burn.

Thus it is established that this movement is necessary to existence, which is either growing or declining. Now, as the spirit continues to exist after death, it necessarily progresses or declines; and in the other world to cease to progress is the same as to decline; but it never leaves its own condition, in which it continues to develop.

'Abdu'l-Bahá: Some Answered Questions, *pg. 233*

This view of an ever-progressing afterlife is radically different from the Christian view of a static heaven or the mindless "oneness" of the New Age Nirvana. It helps put our little slips and flaws into a timeless perspective where they can be smoothed by the Hand of Forgiveness.

A Few Words About Forgiveness:

Another analogy concerning guilt, shame and fear is that they are like railroad tracks. As long as you are heading in the right direction, they keep you in line with very little effort. But if a major test comes along and "derails" you, then guilt and shame can actually act as barriers to getting back "on line." You need love and forgiveness to lift you up and steer you back in the right direction. Here is a little story about how easy it is to receive forgiveness in the Bahá'í Faith - and how unwilling to accept that forgiveness most of us are.

You may have heard the tradition that if you count a certain number of waves in 'Akká then you will receive forgiveness for all of your sins. Well, when I went on pilgrimage, I found the following quotation:

Verily, he that entereth therein ['Akká], longing for it and eager to visit it, God will forgive his sins, both of the past and of the future. And he that departeth from it, other than as a pilgrim, God will not bless his departure.

Bahá'u'lláh: Epistle to the Son of the Wolf, *pg. 178*

I figured that I had, indeed, entered 'Akká with longing, and had departed as a pilgrim, so therefore all my sins were forgiven, both past and future. Isn't that nice? Isn't God kind? Aren't you happy for me?

Would you be surprised to hear that my fellow pilgrims were *not* happy? Indeed, they were, almost without exception, *furious* with me for suggesting that all my sins (and theirs) were forgiven. Our guide was equally adamant that the quotation did not apply to us. They were all concerned that *if I believed that my sins were forgiven before they were even committed, that I would have no motivation to be obedient!* They saw me sidestep the fear of external punishment, and did not believe that my hope of external reward, my internal love of God or my internal sense of shame were powerful enough to prevent me from evil deeds. How sad.

All my sins are forgiven, both past and future Isn't that nice?

I, on the other hand, knew that for me personally, shame, guilt and fear had done more to keep me away from God than my perceived sins ever could. Indeed, I was one of those people who was convinced that I was such a shameful person, that my actions no longer made any difference in the world. When I began to feel loved and forgiven, I decided I wasn't so irrelevant after all!

If you feel you would benefit from a healthy dose of forgiveness, but can't make it to 'Akká any time soon, you might enjoy the following prayers and quotations.

My Favorite Quotations on Forgiveness

My God, my God! If none be found to stray from Thy path, how, then, can the ensign of Thy mercy be unfurled, or the banner of Thy bountiful favor be hoisted? And if iniquity be not committed, what is it that can proclaim Thee to be the Concealer of men's sins, the Ever-Forgiving, the Omniscient, the All-Wise? May my soul be a sacrifice to the trespasses of them that trespass against Thee, for upon such trespasses are wafted the sweet savors of the tender mercies of Thy Name, the Compassionate, the All-Merciful. May my life be laid down for the transgressions of such as transgress against Thee, for through them the breath of Thy grace and the fragrance of Thy loving-kindness are made known and diffused amongst men. May my inmost being be offered up for the sins of them that have sinned against Thee, for it is as a result of such sins that the Day Star of Thy manifold favors revealeth itself above the horizon of Thy bounty, and the clouds of Thy never-failing providence rain down their gifts upon the realities of all created things.

Bahá'u'lláh: Gleanings from the Writings of Bahá'u'lláh, *pp. 310-311*

O Thou the Supreme Word of God! Fear not, nor be Thou grieved, for indeed unto such as have responded to Thy Call, whether men or women, We have assured forgiveness of sins, as known in the presence of the Best Beloved and in conformity with what Thou desirest.

The Báb: Selections from the Writings of the Báb, *pg. 55*

It is seemly that the servant should, after each prayer, supplicate God to bestow mercy and forgiveness upon his parents. Thereupon God's call will be raised: 'Thousand upon thousand of what thou hast asked for thy parents shall be thy recompense!'

The Báb: Selections from the Writings of the Báb, *pg. 94*

O my God! Let the outpourings of Thy bounty and blessings descend upon homes whose inmates have embraced Thy Faith, as a token of Thy grace and as a mark of loving-kindness from Thy presence. Verily unsurpassed art Thou in granting forgiveness.

The Báb: Selections from the Writings of the Báb, *pg. 200*

O Thou forgiving Lord!

Although some souls have spent the days of their lives in ignorance, and became estranged and contumacious, yet, with one wave from the ocean of Thy forgiveness, all those encompassed by sin will be set free. Whomsoever Thou willest Thou makest a confidant, and whosoever is not the object of Thy choice is accounted a transgressor. Shouldst Thou deal with us with Thy justice, we are all naught but sinners and deserving to be shut out from Thee, but shouldst Thou uphold mercy, every sinner would be made pure and every stranger a friend. Bestow, then, Thy forgiveness and pardon, and grant Thy mercy unto all.

Thou art the Forgiver, the Lightgiver and the Omnipotent.

'Abdu'l-Bahá: Bahá'í Prayers *(US edition), pg. 47*

intimacy as a tool for healing shame

After coming to a deeper understanding of healthy shame and forgiving ourselves for our imperfections, we need to take our imperfect selves back into the Community and establish some intimate connections. By intimate, I don't mean "touchy-feely" or sexual. I mean open, honest and loving. This is very different from the fake, superficial "nice-nice" kind of loving relationships we have with Bahá'ís we are trying to fool into thinking we are happy and spiritually content. This is real.

We need to take our imperfect selves back into the Community and establish some intimate connections.

Many years ago, a "perfect" Bahá'í invited me to his house to watch television. He had a perfect body, perfect face, perfect house, perfect job and perfect new wife. Everyone loved him. That is, they loved the "him" they saw. Then he pulled the shades and told me about his addiction to pornography, and his terror that his wife would find out. He knew I did "that therapy stuff" and wanted me to fix him quick. I suggested that he join some 12-step groups, and go into therapy with his wife. From my experience, that is about as quick as it gets.

Unfortunately, he was afraid that other people might find out that he wasn't perfect. His shame convinced him that he was only lovable if he hid behind the mask of perfection. That mask was really a wall. It kept him from experiencing true intimacy with his wife and honest friendship within the Community. His fear of exposure created a feeling of isolation, and it was the fear and isolation, *not* the pornography, that was bound to push him away from the Community and destroy his marriage. His isolation compounded his shame by making him feel that he was the only Bahá'í in the world with this problem. If he could have dropped the mask, he might have been blessed with the knowledge that he was not alone.

Isolation compounds our shame by making us feel that we are the only Bahá'ís in the world with these problems.

Bahá'ís are not perfect. Whatever law you find difficult to follow, several thousand other Bahá'ís have also struggled with it and have failed to follow it for a while. Many are struggling still. There are sex addicts, alcoholics, drug addicts, homosexuals, wife beaters, cross-dressers, politicians, over-eaters, liars, thieves, backbiters, speeders, adulterers, beggars (and even people who still celebrate Easter) right here in the Bahá'í Community. God loves them all. He also loves the people struggling with arrogance, self-centeredness, ego, manipulation, insincerity, anger, aggression, greed, fear, apathy, ignorance, co-dependency and control, though they often cause the greater harm.

The thing to remember is that even though it is particularly difficult to struggle towards the high Bahá'í standard, your chances of eventually succeeding with God's help are much greater than your chance of succeeding alone. If your local Bahá'í Community has successfully overcome its desire to look perfect, then it can be your greatest tool in your struggle to obey God's laws. The more we open up to each other and share the reality of our lives, the easier it will be to replace shame with love as the guiding force in our lives.

How does this work?

The more we open up to each other and share the reality of our lives, the easier it will be to replace shame with love.

Well, lets take one of the most difficult laws in the Bahá'í Community. Sex. Many single Bahá'ís engage in inappropriate sexual interaction. That is thousands and thousands of people - young and old, rich and poor, new Bahá'ís and old-timers. As long as all of the Bahá'ís support the lie that only "bad" Bahá'ís have a problem with this law, where do you think each of these thousands of people will go for support when they find themselves being tested by temptation? They go to their sexually active non-Bahá'í friends of course! Is this helpful? NO!

If we have learned anything from the success of Alcoholics Anonymous and the other 12-step programs, it is that people feel less ashamed of their failures and more hopeful of success when they know that they are not alone. Also, the best people to support your success are the people struggling to succeed alongside you. But for the Bahá'í Community to profit from this knowledge, we must begin to be honest about the struggles we face. This means that we must be free to admit mistakes without fearing retribution.

When an alcoholic tells a fellow recovering alcoholic that he is worried bout relapsing, his comrade does not say, "You know God will get you for that." He says, "Call me when you feel the temptation, and I'll be right over to pray with you and help you be strong."

This is honesty. This is intimacy. This is true Bahá'í love, being expressed by people we might be tempted to exclude from our Community as "undesirable." And it is only possible if we are honest about the things that cause us shame. Ten minutes of shared tears is preferable to ten hours of pious preaching.

So how would we do this with Bahá'ís? Well, if you are a new Bahá'í, you have a unique opportunity to be "real" with your new Bahá'í friends from the start. If you can resist putting up masks, then you can help other Bahá'ís respond honestly to you.

If you are an "old timer," consider rethinking your standard approach to "consolidation." Instead of one more class on chastity for the Bahá'í Youth, for example, why not have the adults tell them the truth about what they really did before they got married. Give them practical advice for avoiding painful situations, train them to understand shame, teach them forgiveness, offer them affection and give them a temptation buddy to call when lust and shame are clouding their vision. Being honest about our failures will allow us to become the family that we claim to be.

I know that this level of intimacy is difficult–especially in larger communities, but I can imagine a time when we have retreats, workshops, support groups and honest friendships that will make true intimacy possible. In the meantime, we can start by being more honest with one another about some of our littler tests. For example, we could stop pretending that the Fast is really easy for most the Bahá'ís. We could admit that we miss the taste of beer, and don't always remember our prayers; that we like celebrating Christian holidays; and sometimes, we even wake up in the middle of the night wondering if there really is a God.

putting law into perspective

A Parable

Here is a story that illustrates and expands on the relationship between law, love, shame and success:

Once there were two children, Justus and Marcy, who read stories to each other every night before they went to bed. They usually read fairy tales and other children's books they found on the shelves in their parent's library, but one day they happened to pick up a copy of "A Midsummer Night's Dream." At first they found it difficult to understand the unusual language, but there was something so enchanting about the story that they couldn't put it down. The next night they looked for more books by Mr. Shakespeare. His language was so beautiful and there seemed to be so many layers of meaning in his works that they both fell in love with his writing. They discovered that reading great literature could be more than just entertaining–it could be inspiring, uplifting and even educational!

Over the course of the next few months a deep yearning began to grow in each of their hearts. They wanted to give back to the world some of the beauty they had received. They wanted to become writers!

Now both Justus and Marcy loved school and were good students, so they went to their teachers and told them their new desire to become writers. You can imagine how pleased their teachers were to discover such motivated students! Justus was two years older than Marcy. His teacher told him that the secret to being a great writer was to understand and follow the laws of grammar. In addition to his regular homework, he was given several grammar worksheets to complete every night. When the rest of the class was given a two-page paper, he would be assigned a five-page paper to give him more practice at writing. Because his teacher knew he loved great literature, he would take favorite sentences out of context and ask Justus to make up his own sentence using the exact same structure, using different words. Justus was excited by all of this extra work. If this is what it takes to be a great writer, he thought, then I am lucky to be able to do it!

Marcy's teacher was also very happy to find such a motivated student. She told Marcy that the secret of being a great writer was to develop a thirst for great literature, to fall in love with the beauty and power of words, and to remain humble in the face of language's capacity to change the world. She asked Marcy to read an extra half-hour every night. She introduced her to new and talented authors, and took a few minutes every day to talk with her about what she was reading. During these times, she would often point out unusual sentences and discuss how the rules of grammar made them easier to understand. When she graded Marcy's papers she would look for recurring errors and explain the grammatical rule that would make her writing more clear. She would not mark a mistake unless it made the sentence harder to understand.

When Justus heard about Marcy's teacher's approach, he felt just a little superior. He believed that it was because he was older that he was being taught how to do it the right way from the beginning. He also believed that he had less time to waste, so he must learn everything as quickly as possible. He took great pride in staying up late to work on his worksheets and extra-long papers. He found he no longer had time to read bedtime stories with his sister, who was working her way through their parent's library at increasing speed.

As I said, Justus was a good student. He was used to getting papers back with very few corrections, just a big, red "A" in the top corner. Now, however, his papers came back covered with red marks. Not only was every single spelling and grammar error circled in red, but the margins were full of comments like "use better word here" or "don't use passive voice." When he saw the "C" at the top of the page, he was so embarrassed that he tried to hide his papers from his friends. The kid behind him whispered, "Boy, I thought I was dumb, but I didn't make nearly as many mistakes as you did."

When he asked his teacher why his grade was so bad, his teacher said, "If you want to be a writer, you have to hold yourself to a higher standard. What was good enough before is no longer acceptable. I used to only mark the bigger mistakes–the ones you should have mastered by now–but now I am showing you how to become a perfect writer. Study these corrections for your next paper."

So Justus studied and studied. In time his papers became better and better, but they were still covered with red marks. In the past, he had shared his papers with his parents, who would put them up on the refrigerator, but now he hid them away in his notebook.

Meanwhile, Marcy was also trying her hand at writing. She wrote fanciful fairy tales and luscious love poems (she was at that age). At the end of each, her teacher would write "Wonderful!" or "Moving" or "You are doing much better at punctuation, now let's work some more on verb tense..." or something like that. Her parents would show these stories to their friends and brag about their budding author.

When Justus read her stories, he could find dozens of mistakes the teacher had missed, but somehow he would get so caught up in the joy of the words that it never seemed to matter. Meanwhile, his own stories seemed to become more and more mechanical. His life was filled with worksheets and homework. What was there for him to write about? When he tried to read Shakespeare, he would find himself either analyzing the structure of the play or comparing his own shallow efforts to the works of this genius. What was the point? Anything he could think to say had already been said much better by someone else.

It didn't take too many months of this to convince Justus that he was not really cut out to be a writer. If there was any talent in his family, it obviously belonged to his sister. He told his teacher that he had changed his mind about being an author, and returned the unfinished workbooks and exercises. From then on, whenever he looked at his teacher, he thought he could see a hint of disappointment on his face. He stopped reading entirely and never talked to his sister about the love for literature they once shared.

Marcy's love for writing grew and grew. The great authors seemed like friends of hers. She would often imagine them looking over her shoulder as she worked on a particularly complex sentence. In trying to perfect her skills, she bought massive reference books that explained the rules of grammar and how they could be applied in different ways. She didn't always follow the rules, and she often made mistakes, but the over-all effect of her stories was inspiring and uplifting to everyone who read them.

Two years later, when she advanced into the class her brother had taken, his teacher told her how happy he was to have a student dedicated to the art of writing. "Your brother," he said sadly, "obviously did not have the great love for literature that you have, or he would not have quit writing so soon."

"You are wrong," she replied. "His love was every bit as great a mine, but you did not fan the fire of his love. If love is a flame, then knowledge is the wood that burns. But the spirit of beauty is like the invisible air that flows through the empty spaces. You filled his mind with so much knowledge of rules and regulations that there was no room for spirit. His love could not breathe. It choked and died. He is not to blame, you are."

The teacher was dismayed by her answer, and responded sarcastically, "Well, if that is your attitude, then you obviously won't want to bother learning the rules of grammar from me."

"Quite the contrary," she said, "in the last two years, I have been given the chance to fill myself with the spirit of beauty. Go ahead. Pile me high with facts, figures, rules and knowledge. I cannot be extinguished. Perhaps someday I can even rekindle my brother."

The moral of the story is simple but it is true. The secret of staying a Bahá'í is to fall in love with Bahá'u'lláh. Love is a state of being in which the experience of virtue is its own reward. When we are intoxicated with the wine of love, when virtue itself makes us swoon with ecstasy, then reward and punishment, right and wrong, rule and regulation become meaningless. We cling to what is good and beautiful because it is all that we can see, feel or hear.

Love is a state of being in which the experience of virtue is its own reward.

Love may be a slower path to knowledge and obedience than a cram-course in Bahá'í Law, but it is a much more permanent path. Even if a new Bahá'í is willing to try to obey every law from the beginning, it is a mistake to make obedience the primary *focus* of our relationship to Bahá'u'lláh. Read the Writings. Study *The Hidden Words*, and as you live the story of your life, you will naturally become curious as to how to live with greater clarity, how to do it better, and yes, how to follow the rules.

The Tongue of My power hath, from the heaven of My omnipotent glory, addressed to My creation these words: "Observe My commandments, for the love of My beauty." Happy is the lover that hath inhaled the divine fragrance of his Best-Beloved from these words, laden with the perfume of a grace which no tongue can describe.

Bahá'u'lláh: The Kitáb-i-Aqdas, *pp. 20-21*

It's Never Too Late to Fall in Love

It is all well and good, you say, to talk about children learning to love Shakespeare, but what if you've already been a Bahá'í for years and you still don't feel that sense of personal connection and love that the "sweetness and light" Bahá'ís obviously already feel? Is it too late? Is love something that you either feel or don't feel, or can you teach yourself how to love?

Let me tell you about something that happened to me that convinced me that my soul can learn how to fall in love with the most unusual things in the most unexpected ways.

When I was a freshman in college, I took a ceramics course and a class on Japanese culture. On the wall of the ceramics studio was a large full-color poster of a lopsided brown clay bowl with a crack in the side. Since I knew something about printing, I thought to myself "who in the world would spend good money to print a color poster of such an ugly pot?" Three months later, I was throwing a cup on the pottery wheel and happened to glance up at the wall. As I returned to my work, I thought to myself "what a beautiful ceramic bowl that is. It is so expressive and has such character." It was, of course, the same ugly bowl I had seen before, but this time my heart had enough experience to appreciate its beauty. You have to understand that, though I had spent three months studying Japanese culture, I had put no thought nor effort into appreciating that particular bowl. My response was purely aesthetic and instinctual, not intellectual.

My point is that your heart is already in the process of falling in love with Bahá'u'lláh. While your intellect is absorbing the facts and figures of Bahá'u'lláh's Writings, your heart is basking in its beauty. One day you will casually "look up" and have your breath taken away by the startling beauty and wonder of His Revelation.

The more you think about it, the harder it may be to see. But when we expose ourselves to beauty, our hearts are trained by it, whether we are aware of it or not.

When we expose ourselves to beauty, our hearts are trained by it, whether we are aware of it or not.

One of the proofs of this unconscious love is this simple test: If someone offered you a new house to forget that Bahá'u'lláh existed, forget all of His prayers and writings, and never hear of Him again, would you do it? Take a moment and observe your reaction to the offer. Are you gleefully touring your imaginary new home in your mind, or is your heart feeling empty and lost at the mere thought of never hearing another *Hidden Word* or saying another *Noonday Prayer*?

a word about the covenant

Whenever the subject of obedience to Bahá'í Law is mentioned, the word "Covenant" surfaces as the apparent "magic fix" to all of our problems. It is. But perhaps not in the way many people imagine it. The "long version" of the Covenant is every word in every one of the Bahá'í Writings. The medium version is available in a 500 page book called *The Covenant of Bahá'u'lláh* which you may want to read someday. Here is my 120 word version. What it lacks in detail, it makes up in simplicity.

When you fall in love with Bahá'u'lláh, you will find yourself attracted to 'Abdu'l-Bahá. When you fall in love with 'Abdu'l-Bahá, you will find yourself attracted to Shoghi Effendi. When you fall in love with Shoghi Effendi, you will want to know all about the Universal House of Justice. When you come to understand the function of the Universal House of Justice, you will come to love the entire Administrative Order.

Love grows into faith and trust. You will naturally want to follow the guidance of Bahá'u'lláh and the Institutions He established, even when their instructions run counter to your desires. In return, the spiritual qualities you love will flow back into your soul allowing it to live forever.

That's it. If at any time you find yourself disliking or distrusting some part of the Bahá'í system, don't panic. Go back to the beginning—your love for Bahá'u'lláh—and see where the love and trust began to get disconnected.

When I was a young Bahá'í, for example, the only thing I knew about Shoghi Effendi was that he wrote that section in *The Advent of Divine Justice* about chastity. I never gave myself the chance to fall in love with him as a source of love and inspiration the way I did with Bahá'u'lláh and 'Abdu'l-Bahá. I fooled myself into thinking that chastity was a "Shoghi Effendi Law" rather than a law of Bahá'u'lláh. This allowed me to mentally break the link between Bahá'u'lláh and Shoghi Effendi, and from there it was easier to break the law. Now that I am old and married, and chastity has taken on a more subtle meaning, I find that I am often awed and inspired by the tenderness and sensitivity with which Shoghi Effendi presented Bahá'u'lláh's laws to an immature Community. It was the shame of my own disobedience that cut me off from the healing understanding he had to offer.

One last clarification of the Covenant: It is not enough to fall in love with Bahá'u'lláh as a really nice, really smart guy. Bahá'u'lláh claims to be a Manifestation of God. He claims to know us and our spiritual needs better than we know ourselves. If you never really come to understand and love Bahá'u'lláh as The Divine Physician, then there will be very little to bind you to the laws of the Covenant when they don't suite your personal desires.

*The Blessing of Principles**

The principles of the Teachings of Bahá'u'lláh should be carefully studied, one by one, until they are realized and understood by mind and heart—so will you become strong followers of the light, truly spiritual, heavenly soldiers of God, acquiring and spreading the true civilization in Persia, in Europe, and in the whole world.

'Abdu'l-Bahá: Paris Talks, *pg. 22*

Armed with understanding, forgiveness, intimacy and love, it is safe to explore the blessing of Bahá'í principles and laws.

Now that you are forearmed and forewarned with understanding, forgiveness, intimacy and love, it is safe to explore the blessing of Bahá'í principles and laws.

In Part 1 of this book, I discussed the external stresses created by the "blessing" of trying to connect with a unique new Community while holding on to your own uniqueness as an individual. Now we will look at some of the internal stresses created by the "blessing" of trying to align your personal moral and social compass with the teachings of the Bahá'í Writings.

You might be thinking, "This is the easy part - I already believed in the Bahá'í principles before I joined." And you might very well be right. But in my experience, most of us join because we were attracted to a particular element of the Faith. You might say the teachings "struck a chord," and we resonated in harmony with them. As we explore the Faith, however, we discover that it really is like an entire piano. It can strike lots of different chords in many different keys. Even though they are all in tune with God's Will, if we don't understand how they fit together, they can sound discordant to our ears and in our hearts.

---

*For a list of Bahá'í Principles, see Appendix 1

One common observation about the Faith is that it combines traditionally "liberal" social principles with traditionally "conservative" moral teachings. Unlike Christianity, which focuses on personal salvation, the Faith has something to say about most of the issues of the day, and these perspectives are presented *in the Writings and/or by a source of Authority*. This means that it is very likely that as you learn more, you will find something in the Writings that will surprise you. Perhaps it will dismay you. It might even outrage you.

As you learn more, you will find something in the Writings that will surprise you.

If this should happen, I encourage you to take a few moments to re-walk the path which first lead you to Bahá'u'lláh. Remember the source, and pray for understanding.

Walking the Maze

Have you ever noticed how much easier it is to work a maze from the end backward to the beginning than the way you are supposed to, from beginning to end? Think of Bahá'u'lláh as the center point in a ring of radiating mazes. Each maze represents a teaching or principle. Some of these "mazes" are easy to follow, while others are hard. When you first became a Bahá'í, you started with some inner belief. You followed this belief through one of the mazes and discovered Bahá'u'lláh as the Generator of that principle. This is the arm of the maze that is easiest for you. You can walk it forward and backward with no doubt or confusion. It is your path of certitude.

Follow this path to Bahá'u'lláh and ask for guidance. Then from *this* central point of faith and assurance, try to follow the twists and turns outward to the external principle. If you start from the point of outrage or confusion and try to pound your way through the walls of the maze from the outside in, then you are likely to become even more confused and frustrated.

For Example? People whose commitment to racial harmony lead them to Bahá'u'lláh might be horrified to discover that the Faith condones the death penalty. By only seeing how this principle is being applied in the U.S. today, they might find it very difficult to imagine this principle serving the Will of God. But if they follow the love of racial harmony to the love of Bahá'u'lláh, they will find in that center a faith in the immortality of the soul, love for justice, and the essence of forgiveness. These teachings make the death penalty an easier principle to understand and accept.

In time, what you will discover is that the more you focus on Bahá'u'lláh, the more interconnected the principles become.

If a conservative Christian followed the path of prophecy to discover Bahá'u'lláh sitting on the throne of Christ, this person could be committed to the Cause of God, but still have difficulty living in a multi-racial Community. Again, from the love of Christ to the love of Bahá'u'lláh, the well-walked path can take the Christian to a place where the oneness of humanity can at least become a possibility.

In time, what you will discover is that the more you focus on Bahá'u'lláh, the more interconnected all the principles become. It is only at the outermost layers of politics and materialism that the principles can be separated at all. Each principle leads to every other principle when the path passes near Bahá'u'lláh.

Of course, the challenge of the principles does not come only from those we don't understand. It also comes from those we understand and accept wholeheartedly and completely, but at which we find ourselves failing miserably on a daily basis. When I say that I practice the Golden Rule, I mean that I *practice* it in hopes that at some point in my life I will get it right!

The greatest challenge of every principle is its daily application. When we become Bahá'ís, it means we have to try to put our hands, our feet *and* our money where our mouth is. On top of that, we have so *many* principles. If the Faith were like all of the "one issue" service clubs out there, it would make life so much easier, but just as we get good at promoting peace, we are asked to promote racial harmony. When we promote racial harmony, we are encouraged to educate children. Then we are challenged to practice material sacrifice!

When we focus too long and hard on only one principle, we can forget our spiritual center and begin to resent those whose focus is elsewhere.

Perhaps we are challenged to address all of these principles simultaneously, because God knows that the only way to succeed is to take that shortcut through the maze and visit Him on our way from one principle to another. Indeed, when we focus too long and hard on only one principle, we can forget our spiritual center and begin to resent those whose focus is elsewhere. I've heard some teachers of children's classes bemoan the fact that more people don't put children first, while some Bahá'í feminists complain that the men have not done enough for women. Some administrators worry that people don't follow procedures, some Bahá'í scholars complain that not enough research is being done, and some black Bahá'ís insist that white Bahá'ís are racist. The list of our human failures goes on forever.

On behalf of all of us imperfect Bahá'ís, I plead guilty on all counts. The principles, when understood correctly, actually include every idea presented in any of the many thousands of translated and untranslated volumes. Their sheer volume is overwhelming. If they are perceived as an obligation, they will inspire guilt, shame and burnout. If perceived as an adventure, however, they become something else entirely.

If Bahá'í principles are perceived as an obligation, they will inspire guilt, shame and burnout. If perceived as an adventure, however, they become something else entirely.

I encourage you to imagine the principle which led you to Bahá'u'lláh as a path which took you from where you were in the world *towards* God. Then imagine the rest of the principles as paths leading *from* God to the rest of the world. **Now go exploring!** Explore prayer and meditation; explore social activism; explore arts and sciences; explore language and mysticism. You will never run out of new things to discover, and you will never be in danger of getting lost—as long as you always start at the center.

From this perspective, it is clear that the Bahá'í Principles include more than the ten or twelve you find on most lists. Go find yourself some more. All you have to do is read any sentence out of any Bahá'í book and rephrase the main idea as a principle. Try this any time you begin to think you "know" the Bahá'í teachings. It's an ocean out there.

*The Blessing of Laws**

Bahá'í laws come from God. They are a material path to a spiritual virtue. If it were easy to see the virtue at the end of the path, and if we were in love with that virtue for its own sake, then not only would the law be easy to follow, but it would be irrelevant. We would obey it whether it was a law or not. But it is not easy to "see the end in the beginning." So the "blessing" of Bahá'í law can easily become the greatest test for both new and old-time Bahá'ís.

This section will focus on helping us understand laws so that we can identify the virtues they were designed to instill in us.

One of the major goals of this book is to make it easier for us all to follow the laws. To do that, I suggest a two step process. First, identify goal virtues, and then increase our love for them. When we can't identify the virtues strengthened by a law, or we don't love that virtue, then we only have our love for Bahá'u'lláh to inspire obedience. Much of this book has been focused on increasing our love for both virtues and Bahá'u'lláh, but sometimes our minds long for more. This section will focus on helping us understand the laws so that we can identify the virtues they were designed to instill in us. This can make obedience more "whole-hearted" and more "whole-minded."

Four Kinds of Laws Squared:

There is not a clear line between principles and laws. That is because laws can be divided into four broad categories:

1. Exhortations - These are essentially expressions of principle as they apply to individual actions. They point in a general direction rather than defining strict boundaries of behavior.

*For a list of Bahá'í Laws, see Appendix 1

2. Laws which are between the individual and God–These include laws like obligatory prayer, fasting, etc. They outline specific behavior, but it is no one's business but your own whether you obey them or not. To some extent, this also includes laws for which there are only sanctions if they are "flagrant," - for example, drinking alone in your own home is between you and God, but public intoxication involves the reputation of the Community.

3. Laws which operate between people, but for which there are no sanctions or punishment – These laws include attendance at Feast, participation in Bahá'í elections, giving to the Fund, etc. These are also no one's business but your own.

4. Laws which involve the Community and for which there are sanctions if they are not obeyed – This includes flagrant use of drugs and alcohol, inappropriate sexual conduct, violation of marriage laws, partisan politics, etc.

You will note that only a small percentage of all the Bahá'í laws are anyone's business but your own.

You will note that only a small percentage of all the Bahá'í laws are anyone's business but your own. What's more, the small percentage that might involve sanctions is only the business of the Spiritual Assembly. If you need to know about it, the Assembly will tell you–not your local gossip. It helps to remember this, whether you are being judged or are tempted to judge others yourself.

I rewrote the above section, to remove the repeated comment that most laws are "no one's business but your own." I feared that I risked sounding snotty or defensive and tried to soften my tone. Then I remembered the story I heard about a "big wig" Bahá'í who publicly humiliated some Bahá'í youth for not standing up straight enough when reading prayers.

While I admit that there may certainly be a problem with posture(ing) in the Community, I don't see it on the list of issues we are obligated to help each other with. Bahá'ís have been asked to work on racism, sexism, child education, world peace, drug, & alcohol abuse and backbiting. There are also individuals in the Community who need assistance in overcoming child abuse, sex addiction, homosexual behavior, co-dependence, domestic violence, incest, cross-dressing, compulsive lying, stealing, over-eating, shopping, TV addiction and gambling. Compassion demands that we also support those who are suffering from mental illness, physical illnesses, poverty, homelessness, infertility, divorce, and the deaths of family and friends.

These are serious issues that cry out for our attention. I hope that my many dear Bahá'í friends will not be too offended if I say that I haven't known a single Bahá'í whose problems were not obviously more serious and urgent than the mild lack of reverence implied by bad posture. It may feel righteous to nit-pick each other to death, but it only succeeds in distracting us from the process of becoming a true Community.

It may feel righteous to nit-pick each other to death, but it only succeeds in distracting us from the process of becoming a true Community.

So do me a favor. Next time someone gets up at Feast or corners you in a meeting and tries to make you feel guilty for not sitting right, standing right, wearing the right clothes, being on time, memorizing prayers, being vegetarian, getting up at dawn - or because you *did* read a prayer in the bathroom, kissed someone, said damn, watched a violent movie or stayed home from Feast...

Just giggle.

We don't have time for petty tyranny.

And we don't have big wigs - just Bahá'ís.

Just Bahá'ís who need each other, and need each other's love and understanding.

Desperately.

So,

moving on,

there are four *different* categories into which laws might fall, when considered from a personal standpoint.

A. Laws that make perfect sense and are easy to follow.

B. Laws that you just don't understand, but don't really apply to your daily life anyway, so you can ignore them.

C. Laws that make sense, but which seem to stand right in the way of your hopes, habits and desires.

D. Laws that you really don't understand, and are so different from your experience and habit that they are hard to remember or follow.

You can find anything from an exhortation which makes sense and is easy to follow to a sanctionable law which you don't understand and is hard to follow.

If we crisscross these two sets of categories, you can get anything from an exhortation which makes sense and is easy to follow to a sanctionable law which you don't understand and is hard to follow.

If we were to survey every person who joined the Bahá'í Faith and then decided to resign, they would fall into three categories. The first would be people who really didn't understand what they were getting into in the first place. I can't do much for them except offer better, more accurate introductory materials.

The second would be people who love Bahá'u'lláh, but are so disappointed in the community that they leave in frustration. I hope that the first part of this book helps them find a balance between love, expectations and forgiveness.

The third group of people are also frustrated and disappointed, but this time with themselves. I suspect that the majority of them would list a law or principle which they didn't understand or agree with as a major contributing factor. This is why I will discuss laws that might not make sense to you later in this section. But before I move forward in that direction, I want to say that I don't believe this is the real reason why these people leave.

I believe that people leave the Faith because they feel ashamed of their inability to live up to the laws and principles that they *do* understand. This is why I wrote so much about understanding shame earlier.

It is the laws that reinforce shame spirals that are usually at the heart of people's rejection of the Faith.

You see, it is hard to feel too much shame and guilt for doing something that you really don't think is wrong. Guilt and shame come from knowing that something is harmful, degrading, stupifying, obsessive, compulsive, cruel or dishonest, and not being able to stop yourself from doing it anyway. It makes you feel unworthy. It makes you feel unforgivable. It makes you want to get away from the sweet, loving Bahá'ís who make you feel like it should be easy to be better.

It is the laws that reinforce shame spirals that are usually at the heart of these people's rejection of the Faith. If they could change their behavior easily, they would. If their behavior did not violate Bahá'í law, then they would not feel the need to distance themselves from us.

Because their leaving is motivated by shame, they must hide the real reason. They must distract themselves and us from the real issues they are struggling with.

So Bahá'ís use the laws that they don't understand as wedges to pry themselves away from the Faith. The heterosexual woman insists that she left the Faith because she didn't agree with the Faith's position on homosexuality, while the father of two decides that if the Faith doesn't support abortion rights, then it can't be of God.

Bahá'ís use the laws that they don't understand as wedges to pry themselves away from the Faith.

When you hear these things, or more important, when you begin to *feel* these things, stop and ask yourself what is really going on. It is very likely that it was your *heart* not your *head* that drew you into the Faith, so if you ever feel yourself pulling away, ask you *heart* what it is that scared you. Is it this law, or some other that is really the issue? Is your anger really anger, or just a mask for fear? If you fear punishment, then are you already secretly punishing yourself with shame, resentment and isolation?

It would be better to return to love and try to heal your concerns from there. Remember that love, understanding, forgiveness, and intimacy are the tools for growth.

Wrestling with Laws We Don't Understand

Disclaimer: *As I begin a presentation of some of the more difficult aspects of the Faith, I thought it would be a good time to remind the reader that, except for direct quotations from the Writings, the opinions expressed in this book are those of an individual, not an institution. The principle of Independent Investigation of the Truth still applies.*

Will you throw this book away in horror if I admit to you that when the authorized translation of *The Kitáb-i-Aqdas* was published in 1992, there were large sections of it that made absolutely no sense to me? I really wanted to talk with other Bahá'ís about what it all meant to them, but they all seemed to understand it perfectly. They talked about how sweet and loving and beautiful it was, and how they wanted to send it out to seekers and political leaders. "Give it to seekers!" I shuddered. After 19 years as a Bahá'í, I was confused by it. What would a seeker think? Or was it just me? Was I a spiritual dwarf? Was I from another planet? I struggled with these questions for a long time, and finally began to see things from a different perspective.

Now the laws that make sense to you may not be *easy* to follow, but at least they don't make you question your faith. And the laws that trouble you might not be the ones that confused me. But whatever the laws are that you have questions about, there is at least a chance that they will make more sense to you when looked at from one of these five perspectives:

1. They were written for people at a different developmental level.
2. They are taking a "back door" approach to a problem.
3. They are taking a pragmatic rather than an ideal approach.
4. They are taking a spiritual rather than a logical approach.
5. They are taking a global rather than a Western approach.

Note that I am not including the catch-all, "That law was written for 100 years ago." It is too easy to dismiss laws as irrelevant when there may be times, places and situations even in our own lives when the principles involved are all too relevant.

1. understanding laws written for people at different developmental levels

I will start with the law that struck me as the most incomprehensible in order to explain the first of these ideas.

> *"Should the garb of anyone be visibly sullied, his prayers shall not ascend to God, and the celestial Concourse will turn away from him."*
>
> *Bahá'u'lláh:* The Kitáb-i-Aqdas, *pg. 47*

Why and to whom was this law written?

Since the Bábís said prayers with Bahá'u'lláh in the "Black Pit" while surrounded by their own waste, I found it difficult to believe that some dust on my shirt would invalidate my prayers. At the same time, I certainly don't enjoy wearing dirty clothes. So I had to ask myself *why* did He write this, and, perhaps more enlightening, to *whom* was He writing this? What kind of person needs to be threatened with punishment in order to inspire a commitment to cleanliness?

Kohlberg, Piaget and Human Development:

Earlier I said that some people are motivated by fear of punishment, others are motivated by hope for reward, and, ideally, some are motivated by the love of God. While this idea is incorporated implicitly in the teachings of the world's religions, an explicit system for studying our moral impulses was proposed by a psychologist named Kohlberg. He divided moral thinking into six stages. Briefly, these are: 1) Fear of punishment; 2) Hope for pleasure; 3) Desire to please peers; 4) Desire to please authority; 5) Commitment to social principles or moral contracts; and 6) Commitment to self-determined moral principles/individual conscience. Other, higher levels (what we might consider spiritual levels) are still under debate.*

Kohlberg divided moral thinking into six stages.

As Bahá'ís, we may be inclined to assume that most adults are motivated by stages five and six. We often feel nervous about the concept of punishment - as though it were an unnecessary evil, applicable to the least enlightened few. Kohlberg found, however, that only about 10% of a sampling of 24 year-olds operated in the higher two stages. Even those of us who like to think of ourselves as morally advanced don't necessarily maintain our moral high ground when put under stress. Each stage builds on the one before, and as we face difficult moral tests, they can collapse upon one another until we land on one strong enough to hold us up. We can be grateful if the fear of God acts as a safety net to catch us before we morally "hit bottom."

What this means is that we are surrounded by people who are at vastly different stages in their moral thinking - but that is not the only way in which people differ.

---

*Some argue that these stages apply more to males than females, but it is the concept of stages, not the specific stages or their order that is important to the poit being made.

People also use different kinds of logic. I know that sounds trite, but it is true on a more fundamental level than most people realize. Some of these differences are cultural, while others are developmental. What does that mean? Well, as we pass through infancy, childhood and adolescence, we do not just learn and grow, we actually change our thinking processes from ego-centric to concrete to *formal* (what I call *abstract*). Even though, as adults, we have grown through each of these stages, it is almost impossible for us to "think backwards" - that is, to try to remember what it felt like to "think like a child."

People use different kinds of logic.

For example: Infants see the whole world as an extension of themselves. People and things only exist as objects of their perception. So when you play "peek-a-boo" with toddlers, they think you can't see them if they can't see you! The concept of "object permanence" is not yet formed.

As they grow older, the sense that "everything is an extension of me" is expressed in anthropomorphic thinking - which is a fancy way of saying that children assume that animals, dolls and even rocks have human personalities.

The capacity to imagine things from outside of one's own perception comes much later in life than we might assume. For example, a seven-year old who knows his or her right and left hand will often be unable to guess which is *your* right hand.

By ten, the logic of daily life–addition and subtraction, cause and effect, symbols and relationships have been mastered, and so they seem deceptively adult. They have acquired "concrete operations," but at this age children cannot yet deal with the *hypothetical.* Concepts and logic that are rooted in abstract logic with no concrete reference are impossible for them.

Part of the turmoil of adolescence is the awakening of abstract reasoning. Who am I? What is God? What if...? Teenagers are capable of asking these kinds of questions on a profound level for the first time. While they often think that they are rebelling against their parents' answers, they may only be rebelling against their own concrete, childish understandings of these answers.

A very important point to make here is that not every adolescent makes the transition from concrete to abstract thinking, and not everyone who does stays there. There are many adults functioning quite well in the world without ever pondering the abstract, or even trying to see things from another's perspective. Likewise, just because abstract reasoning is the one psychologists have labeled "adult thinking" doesn't mean that there might not be many more ways of thinking that the human race has not yet achieved in sufficient fullness to measure. After all, Bahá'ís say that the world is going through adolescence. How could we measure a maturity of thought greater than that of humanity as a whole?

So what do the stages of mental development have to do with Bahá'í law? Consider this: a wise parent or teacher does not project onto children adult motivations or logic, but rather teaches them appropriate actions and guides them towards the next level of understanding.

If we take a look at religious history, we can see that, like wise parents, the Prophets have taught us proper actions, and then guided us to more mature logic. In the teachings of Abraham and Moses, especially, you can see the efforts to guide a community whose members, on average, were in early stages of both moral and logical development. (Idols, for example, are signs of anthropomorphic thinking.)

Christ, building on Their success, worked very hard to give us a taste of abstract rather than concrete thinking. From his followers' questions about wives in heaven and crawling into their mother's womb in order to be born again, it is clear that He had a difficult job to do.

My personal belief is that throughout history, there have been adults operating at every level of both moral and logical development, but as time advanced, the balance shifted higher and higher. The prophets tailored their messages to elevate the thinking of the masses, capture the imaginations of the spiritually insightful, and strike the fear of God into the morally weak.

Bahá'u'lláh must deliver a message that speaks to people of every possible level of development.

Now we come back to Bahá'u'lláh and *The Kitáb-i-Aqdas.* Because of His place in history, His followers have the potential to be the most morally and intellectually advanced in history. But because He is the Universal Manifestation, speaking for the first time to the entire world, He must deliver a message that speaks to people of every possible level of development—both above mine and below mine. This makes it very difficult for me to understand all of the laws. When Bahá'u'lláh speaks to me as though I am a child, addressing concrete issues that are obvious to me and threatening punishment for disobedience, then I feel offended and wonder how He could be speaking to the people of the 21st century.* When he writes of burning arsonists or executing murderers, I am horrified. On the other hand, when he waxes mystical and speaks of the hidden secrets of the maids of heaven, I feel overwhelmed and confused.

---

*Most Christian fundamentalism is based on concrete-operational logic and fear-based morality. If we are ashamed of Bahá'u'lláh's teachings that address this stage, we cannot reach these people.

I have to understand that it is Bahá'u'lláh's job to guide the moral and spiritual development of *all* of humanity—from jungle natives to philosophy professors—for the next thousand years or so. Our job is to look for the insight and guidance that will help *us* move to the next level of our personal development. With hundreds of books in addition to *The Kitáb-i-Aqdas* to read, you might think it would be difficult to find the ideas that speak to your level of understanding. In practice, however, it is fairly easy because we "self-select." We spend our lives looking through the filter of our developmental level. Just as it is impossible for a five-year-old to imagine what kinds of questions a teenager thinks about, we tend to filter out all the laws and teachings that don't match our understanding. Perhaps this explains why so few of my friends were disturbed by the laws of *The Kitáb-i-Aqdas*—they simply didn't see them!

We spend our lives looking through the filter of our developmental level.

So back to my original question: who needs to be told that it is good to wash their clothes? Who will read this law and feel that it was written to them? The guy down the street? A farmer in Africa? My teenage son? Me? I don't know, but perhaps the threat of unanswered prayers will be just the push we need to be more conscientious about cleanliness.

One last comment on cleanliness specifically: A year or so ago the newspapers, my science magazine and even National Public Radio had long articles about a newly researched technique for reducing the spread of disease. It was... (drum roll please) washing your hands! Since a large percentage of the world's population believes in an invisible God while being unaware of invisible germs, this law will promote global health.

2. Understanding Laws that Take an Indirect Approach to a Problem

There are many times in life when the shortest path from where we are to where we want to be is not necessarily a straight line. God knows this much better than we do. Consequently, we sometimes find ourselves trying to resist a law or principle that seems to be running perpendicular to our goal. The "back door" version of this technique is illustrated quite well in the movie "Karate Kid." When the main character asks the "wise master" to teach him karate, he is given the chores of painting the old man's fence and polishing his car. It is only later that he realizes that these "irrelevant" tasks have trained his muscles to respond automatically to various karate moves.

A more subtle, indirect approach was described to me by my Women's History professor in college. According to her, the second president of the Women's Christian Temperance Union, Frances Willard, was not particularly interested in the temperance issue. Her real goal was to get women the vote. Unfortunately, most good Christian women in the 1870s were not interested in voting. They were, however, very interested in keeping their husbands from coming home drunk! By focusing attention on the good, moral, Christian issue of temperance, she convinced millions of women that it was their moral duty to seek the vote so that they could vote against alcohol abuse. She thus trained thousands of women to be effective in the realm of politics, social organization and public speaking. Her indirect approach reached the average woman in ways that the more strident, forceful suffragette movement never could.

Parents use an even more subtle technique of re-direction every day. Instead of saying to a child, "Put on your socks!" many parents will ask, "Do you want to wear your white socks or pink socks today?" This approach avoids unnecessary confrontation by moving the focus off of the requirement and onto the choice.

It is impossible for me, as a human, to know what God's hidden goals were.

Of course, it is impossible for me, as a human, to know what God's hidden goals were when specific laws were made. I can, however, look for secondary benefits for laws that otherwise do not make much sense to me. My favorite example of this is the dowry laws. From a Western perspective this is an outdated custom that can be perceived as the "purchasing" of wives. What might Bahá'u'lláh have been trying to do?

Consider this simple fact. When Bahá'u'lláh wrote the laws concerning the dowry, the majority of the cultures of the world practiced it in some form. At the same time, no major country or culture gave married women the right to own property separately from their husbands. (Variations of this injustice underlie the plot of many great Jane Austin stories).

It was customary for dowries to be paid either to the family of the bride (in countries where women were scarce) or to the family of the husband (in countries where women were plentiful). Bahá'u'lláh took this common custom and turned it upside down to guarantee the wife an independent cache of money that her husband did not control. Why didn't men become outraged at the idea of wives owning property? Perhaps it was because the idea of the dowry seemed so familiar to them, and perhaps it was because their egos were distracted by the choice of whether to pay in silver or gold.

There are other secondary benefits to the dowry laws, like forcing the husband to plan ahead and have a job and be responsible, but it is the more subtle, indirect benefits that I find most fascinating and give me the most faith that Bahá'u'lláh knows what He is doing.

3. understanding laws that take a pragmatic approach to a problem

This idea is perhaps one of the hardest for us idealistic Bahá'ís to accept. Many of us are pragmatic about other aspect of our lives, but when it comes to the Faith, we just want it to work like magic. We want to walk from here straight into the New World Order without having to take into account our immaturity, rebelliousness, diversity or history of failure. We can understand slight diversions of the "back door" approach–take two steps to the left before moving forward to the goal. But when we are told we can't walk east from New York to Haifa–that we will have to walk west across Canada, Alaska, the Bering Strait, Russia and the Middle East to get to that Holy Place, then we are sure that God has made some kind of mistake.

The fact is, all of the Prophets have been incredibly pragmatic. The whole concept of Progressive Revelation is that They only told us what we were ready to grasp. That means that, in retrospect, some of the things they told us were not 100% of the truth.

One example of Bahá'u'lláh's pragmatism can be seen in the *lack* of a law against smoking. The Báb forbade smoking, but (I have been told) the Bábís were the only Persian men who did not smoke. When Bahá'u'lláh forbade us to kill for our religion, he removed the prohibition against smoking so that the Bahá'ís could not be easily identified and martyred. So as bad as smoking is, there was a pragmatic choice between killing millions of future Bahá'ís slowly through cancer, or killing thousands of current Bahá'ís through persecution.

So do Bahá'í scholars now argue that smoking must be a good thing–that there is a spiritual reason to allow smoking? No. It was a pragmatic law, not an ideal one.

Being realistic about what the Bahá'í world is really ready for helps me put into perspective the need to balance ideal goals with pragmatic methods. You might find other laws that make more sense to you when seen as a practical human path rather than an idealistic eagle's flight. I discuss a second one in Appendix 2.

4. Understanding Laws That Take a Spiritual Approach

There are many laws that, while involving outward action, seem to have an intrinsically spiritual quality. These are easier for me to accept, but not necessarily any easier to understand. Prayer, fasting, giving to the Fund, I just assume that these are doing me more good than might be obvious by outward appearances. Some of them, however, seem so ritualized that they nag at my logical side. One such law is the requirement to say Allah'u'Abhá ninety-five times each day. I am obviously not the only one who thinks it sounds strange. I was reading a Christian commentary on the Faith in a bookstore and it used this law to make fun of the idea of progressive revelation. It said "If laws are given to suit the needs of the time, what is so different about today that we would need to say this word 95 times now, and not in Jesus' time?" I was embarrassed that they had successfully found a law to make fun of that I didn't understand.

Imagine my surprise when I read that Dr. Herbert Benson, a non-Bahá'í professor of medicine at Harvard Medical School (and author of *The Relaxation Response*) recommends a form of meditation in which you choose a word or phrase from your religion: Repeat the word or phrase silently to yourself, coordinating it with your breathing... and maintain your focus for at least 10 minutes every day.

As the book went on to describe the physical, mental and spiritual benefits of this exercise, I realized that it was exactly what the "Divine Physician" had ordered. It also seems that previous messengers *had* encouraged various forms of this kind of meditation. It was only the specific word that Bahá'u'lláh had prescribed for this age.

This is just one example of when God's spiritual logic proved to be much more effective than my material logic. I am sure you will find many more examples of laws that fit into this category. I hope you have as much fun finding spiritual validation for them as I have.

God's spiritual logic proved to be much more effective than my material logic.

5. Understanding Laws that Take a Global Approach

I won't say too much about this because it has been hinted at in most of the other points I've made. It is easy to say that a law was designed for 19th century Persia, but it is more accurate to say that the laws were designed for the very diverse world we live in today. Those of us with chlorinated water and indoor plumbing have to remember that more people die every year from curable diseases related to poor sanitation than from cancer or heart disease. Also, most of the world's population is functionally illiterate, and gathering wood to heat water is still a significant job for many women. How can I even begin to understand the ways in which Bahá'u'lláh's laws will help solve these problems when I have never experienced them myself?

The fact is that it will take many generations to establish Bahá'u'lláh's New World Order. It is likely that it will be the laws that I *don't* understand that will make the biggest difference for the most people.

The Burden of Maturity

I hope that you have found these explanations of some of the possible rationale for some of the more controversial laws helpful and enlightening. If they increase your faith, deepen your certitude and make obedience easier, then they have served their purpose. But be warned. They come with a heavy responsibility.

You become responsible for making wise, mature and considered choices as to which of the Bahá'í Writings you are going to take literally.

Once you acknowledge the possibility that not all of what Bahá'u'lláh and 'Abdu'l-Bahá said should be taken literally and at face value, then you become responsible for making wise, mature and considered choices as to which of the Bahá'í Writings you are going to take literally and which you are going to interpret personally. It is this responsibility that made many people uncomfortable with this book when it was first published. It is so much easier to take the fundamentalist perspective of "God said it. I believe it. End of story."

For me, I have no choice. It is impossible for me to believe in grace, mercy and the immortality of the soul and also believe that a dirty shirt will nullify my prayers. I just can't do both. To try would only generate a level of cognitive dissonance that would disrupt my entire being. To me, whole volumes speak of Bahá'u'lláh's grace and mercy, and only one line speaks of dirt and prayers. To remain true to my connection to Bahá'u'lláh, I have to choose the volumes and find a way to interpret the line about dirt and prayers in a new and creative way.

But once I've done that, I run face-first into all sorts of other questions, paradoxes and difficult topics that I am forced to investigate, ponder and interpret for myself.

Oh dear... Interpretation. Isn't that illegal? No. Actually, it is required. Only 'Abdu'l-Bahá and Shoghi Effendi were allowed to interpret the Writings of Bahá'u'lláh for *other* people, but each of us is required to interpret them for ourselves.

Why is that?

No one on earth can tell you precisely what the Bahá'í teachings mean.

There is no one alive on earth who can tell you precisely what the Bahá'í teachings mean or what the Bahá'í community will ultimately look like. All any of us can do is offer our current understandings and observations based on our personal study of the Bahá'í Sacred Writings. Shoghi Effendi himself proclaimed our limited ability to comprehend the secrets of this Cause or predict its future when he said:

> *"All we can reasonably venture to attempt is to strive to obtain a glimpse of the first streaks of the promised Dawn that must, in the fullness of time, chase away the gloom that has encircled humanity. All we can do is to point out, in their broadest outlines, what appear to us to be the guiding principles underlying the World Order of Bahá'u'lláh,...."*
>
> *(Shoghi Effendi, The World Order of Baha'u'llah, p. 34)*

Our efforts at carving our current understanding of Bahá'í teachings into stone are further frustrated by Bahá'u'lláh's reference to an Islamic tradition that says: *"We speak one word, and by it we intend one and seventy meanings; each one of these meanings we can explain." (Bahá'u'lláh, The Kitab-i-Iqan, p. 255)* In other words, every word of revelation has 71 different possible meanings. This means, that the six-word phrase "I knew My love for thee," for example, could have over a hundred billion possible combinations of meanings. That's a lot more possible meanings than there are people on earth. What this means *to me* is that each of us must decide what Bahá'u'lláh wants us to get out of His words. Do I want to take every word of the Writings literally and insist that there are 128,100,283,921 meanings in a six-word sentence, or am I content with the knowledge that there are more than two meanings – at least one of which is *not* literal?

As I quoted before, "We all have a right to our opinions." Once we acknowledge our right to choose among the many *correct* meanings of each sentence, then we must also give people the right to be wrong—because even with 128,100,283,921 correct meanings, there are still several zillion incorrect ones—and no one knows which they are.

Sad but true.

Bahá'ís have to learn to agree to disagree

This means that Bahá'ís have to learn to agree to disagree—even on points of theology and principle that are very near and dear to their hearts—in order to maintain the central principle of unity in diversity. The alternatives are either unity in uniformity or disunity in diversity—neither of which would be good for the community.

If you think I'm being flippant, I'm not. All of this sounds so sweet and obvious until someone comes up with an interpretation that really gets your goat or questions your assumptions. Perhaps it is about free will after death, or the infallibility of the Universal House of Justice, or the organization of the future World Order, or homosexuality, or Ruhi Institutes, or reincarnation, or the importance of scholarship or the value of grace itself.

It's a complex world. Right now, right under your nose, in this non-political religion of ours, there are little power struggles going on over these and many other issues. And if we don't come to our senses soon, and cut everyone a little slack, and remember why we all became Bahá'ís in the first place, then we will all suffer.

As Bahá'ís, we are simply not allowed to argue over theology, but we *are* allowed to express unpopular opinions with tact, wisdom and respect.

"A clear distinction is made in our Faith between authoritative interpretation and the interpretation or understanding that each individual arrives at for himself from his study of its teachings. While the former is confined to the Guardian, the latter, according to the guidance given to us by the Guardian himself, should by no means be suppressed. In fact such individual interpretation is considered the fruit of man's rational power and conducive to a better understanding of the teachings, provided that no disputes or arguments arise among the friends and the individual himself understands and makes it clear that his views are merely his own.

From a letter of the Universal House of Justice to an individual believer, May 27, 1966, Lights of Guidance, p. 311

When disputes or arguments do arise, it is tempting to blame the person whose opinion is most controversial. In doing so, we are actually joining the battle to decide who is right and who is wrong, when (I believe) the real question is *who is claiming authority inappropriately*? Authoritative interpretation "*is confined to the Guardian*," and has not been transferred to any institution. The Guardian is no longer with us, so anyone who claims to know "the truth" is overstepping his authority, no matter how long they've been a Bahá'í, how educated or scholarly they are, what country they are from, or what institution they represent. Remember this when you hear controversial ideas being suppressed in the name of God. Freedom of expression (I believe) is not just an American ideal, but is a Bahá'í ideal, as long as it is tempered with humility.

The essential part of being a Baha'i is *not* the theology, but living the life, loving God and loving one another. All the rest is window dressing.

Let it go.

Living the Life

The goal of surviving the stress of change, adopting the structure of the Community, getting to know the people of the Community, studying the Bahá'í Principles and obeying the laws is to fall in love with Bahá'u'lláh and to live the life He calls us to.

Falling in love and living the life. These two are inseparable. Bahá'u'lláh uses slightly different words in the following quotation, but it means basically the same thing:

Falling in love and living the life. These two are inseparable.

The first duty prescribed by God for His servants is the recognition of Him Who is the Dayspring of His Revelation and the Fountain of His laws, Who representeth the Godhead in both the Kingdom of His Cause and the world of creation. Whoso achieveth this duty hath attained unto all good; and whoso is deprived thereof hath gone astray, though he be the author of every righteous deed. It behoveth everyone who reacheth this most sublime station, this summit of transcendent glory, to observe every ordinance of Him Who is the Desire of the world. These twin duties are inseparable. Neither is acceptable without the other. Thus hath it been decreed by Him Who is the Source of Divine inspiration.

Bahá'u'lláh: The Kitáb-i-Aqdas, *pg. 19*

So how do we do that? Is it a mechanical process of signing a contract and obsessively checking off a list of laws as they are obeyed, or is there something more mystical involved?

Here is a little story that helps bring this somewhat overwhelming concept of love down to more practical terms:

Five men were sitting at a table having lunch when one man looks at his glass and said "You know, I really love to drink water. Nothing else makes me feel as refreshed and satisfied as a cool cup of pure water."

"Well," said one companion, "if you love water, you should really direct your love towards the river, which is the source of all of the water in this city."

"Ahh," said a second, "but the river is fed by the rain and snow in the mountains nearby, so you should really be loving the rain that falls from the heavens."

"Yes," chimed in the third, "but of course, this rain itself comes from the water that evaporated from the ocean to the West, so it is the Ocean we should thank for our blessings."

"But," exclaimed the last, "it is the really the light of the Sun that starts the whole process in motion and keeps the water from remaining frozen and hard, so it is the Sun you should love."

With that, the four philosophers heartily agreed and congratulated themselves on recognizing the true source of their many blessings.

Then the first man smiled at his friends and said. "You are, of course, absolutely correct, and I do love the river, the rain, the ocean and the sun with all the strength of my mind. But it is water that I hold in my hand, and it is water that I will love with my heart, my tongue and my body." With that, he lifted his cup and drank until it was empty.

Loving the Water

When people talk about loving God, they are usually talking about loving *GOD* (the Unknowable Essence), the Holy Spirit, or the Manifestations of God. On rare occasions, Bahá'ís and some New Age thinkers will talk about the importance of loving ourselves as "reflections of God." All of these are wonderful objects of our love, but they are also pretty far beyond our ability to comprehend. Even learning to love our own selves is a pretty abstract concept when presented as a whole.

"Know, verily, that the soul is a sign of God, a heavenly gem whose reality the most learned of men hath failed to grasp, and whose mystery no mind, however acute, can ever hope to unravel."
Bahá'u'lláh: Gleanings, Pages: 158-159

So trying to ascertain whether or not we have succeeded in "loving God" on this abstract level is almost impossible. The attempt can leave us feeling inadequate, confused and defeated.

So if God, the Holy Spirit, the Manifestations, and our own souls are the Sun, Ocean, Rain and River respectively, what is the water that both interacts with all of these levels and is still tangible enough for us to get our minds, hands and hearts around on a personal level?

Virtues.

Loving God is loving the virtues of God.

Yes, plain old-fashioned virtues—virtues that you can define, demonstrate, practice, and even fall in love with. The word "virtues" doesn't have all the supernatural, metaphysical mystery that the phrase "love of God" carries with it, but when it gets down to the nitty-gritty, it means the same thing. Loving God is loving the virtues of God.

When we love virtues, *long* for virtues, develop a true thirst for virtues, then we are loving God. Though this can be difficult, it is much easier to grasp than some of the more mystical or legalistic approaches to the subject.

So how do we develop a thirst for virtues? I thought you'd never ask.

The Bahá'í Writings almost never offer us a "1, 2, 3" list of how to be Bahá'ís, so when I found the following quotation by 'Abdu'l-Bahá, I was thrilled to see just how simple and straight-forward the process could be. It changed my life.

The first thing to do is to acquire a thirst for Spirituality, then Live the Life! Live the Life! Live the Life!

The first thing to do is to acquire a thirst for Spirituality, then Live the Life! Live the Life! Live the Life! The way to acquire this thirst is to meditate upon the future life. Study the Holy Words, read your Bible, read the Holy Books, especially study the Holy Utterances of Bahá'u'lláh; Prayer and Meditation, take much time for these two. Then will you know this Great Thirst, and then only can you begin to Live the Life!

'Abdu'l-Bahá: Star of the West Vol. 19, No. 3, *pg. 69*

If we substitute the phrase "love of virtues" for the phrase "thirst for Spirituality" then the four tools that 'Abdu'l-Bahá outlines begin to make a great deal of sense. The first reminds us of the eternal value of virtues, while the next two expose our hearts to beautiful descriptions of virtues and the last invites us to contemplate the application of these virtues in our daily lives. There is, of course, much more to these tools than this, so I would like to take a few pages to explore them individually. They are 1) Meditate on the Afterlife, 2) Study the Writings, 3) Pray, and 4) Meditate.

Meditate on the Afterlife

Contemplating life after death forces us to think of ourselves as spirits, rather than bodies, and encourages us to consider the virtues and attributes that we will need for growth in the next world. Our vision of our own reality is exalted, and at the same time, our pride over physical accomplishments is exposed as irrelevant. Only our virtues will survive, only our acts of selfless service will be remembered. Will they be enough?

Therefore, in this world he must prepare himself for the life beyond. That which he needs in the world of the Kingdom [Heaven] must be obtained here. Just as he prepared himself in the world of the matrix [womb] by acquiring forces necessary in this sphere of existence, so, likewise, the indispensable forces of the divine existence must be potentially attained in this world.

What is he in need of in the Kingdom which transcends the life and limitation of this mortal sphere? That world beyond is a world of sanctity and radiance; therefore, it is necessary that in this world he should acquire these divine attributes. In that world there is need of spirituality, faith, assurance, the knowledge and love of God. These he must attain in this world so that after his ascension from the earthly to the heavenly Kingdom he shall find all that is needful in that eternal life ready for him.

That divine world is manifestly a world of lights; therefore, man has need of illumination here. That is a world of love; the love of God is essential. It is a world of perfections; virtues, or perfections, must be acquired. That world is vivified by the breaths of the Holy Spirit; in this world we must seek them. That is the Kingdom of everlasting life; it must be attained during this vanishing existence.

By what means can man acquire these things? How shall he obtain these merciful gifts and powers? First, through the knowledge of God. Second, through the love of God. Third, through faith. Fourth, through philanthropic deeds. Fifth, through self-sacrifice. Sixth, through severance from this world. Seventh, through sanctity and holiness. Unless he acquires these forces and attains to these requirements, he will surely be deprived of the life that is eternal. But if he possesses the knowledge of God, becomes ignited through the fire of the love of God, witnesses the great and mighty signs of the Kingdom, becomes the cause of love among mankind and lives in the utmost state of sanctity and holiness, he shall surely attain to second birth, be baptized by the Holy Spirit and enjoy everlasting existence.

'Abdu'l-Bahá : The Promulgation of Universal Peace, pg. 226

study the holy words

When the subject of reading the Writings comes up, there is one quotation that is usually thrown out to impress upon us the critical nature of this obligation:

Recite ye the verses of God every morn and eventide. Whoso faileth to recite them hath not been faithful to the Covenant of God and His Testament, and whoso turneth away from these holy verses in this Day is of those who throughout eternity have turned away from God. Fear ye God, O My servants, one and all.

Bahá'u'lláh: The Kitáb-i-Aqdas, *pp. 73*

This quotation is certainly enough to strike the fear of God into all of us who fall short of this duty. But the quotation does not stop there, and it is the "*rest of the story*" so to speak, that I would like to explore in the context of acquiring our "thirst for spirituality." Bahá'u'lláh goes on to say:

Pride not yourselves on much reading of the verses or on a multitude of pious acts by night and day; for were a man to read a single verse with joy and radiance it would be better for him than to read with lassitude [weariness] all the Holy Books of God, the Help in Peril, the Self-Subsisting. Read ye the sacred verses in such measure that ye be not overcome by languor and despondency. Lay not upon your souls that which will weary them and weigh them down, but rather what will lighten and uplift them, so that they may soar on the wings of the Divine verses towards the Dawning-place of His manifest signs; this will draw you nearer to God, did ye but comprehend.

Bahá'u'lláh: The Kitáb-i-Aqdas, *pp. 73-74*

With the entire quotation in mind, I would like to consider again how it is that we *fall in love with Bahá'u'lláh.*

Falling in Love with Bahá'u'lláh

As I have said throughout this book, the secret of obeying the laws, the secret of staying a Bahá'í, the secret of being happy, the secret of life itself is to fall in love with Bahá'u'lláh.

So how do you do that?

Contrary to popular opinion, love is rarely a thunderbolt out of the sky. It is, rather, a hundred million tiny raindrops that fill us up and sweep us out to the ocean. It is the result of small, repeating positive interactions. It is knowledge born of consistent contact. It is a flame that must be fed tiny twigs before being given sturdy sticks or large logs.

Think of all of the people you love even though you have never met them. Yes, you! We fall in love with strangers every day—from poets to pop stars—we form unbreakable bonds with those whose capacity for heart-to-heart communication transcends the need for eye-to-eye contact. I love James Taylor, for example, because I have been moved by his music every day for weeks or months at a time. I can only imagine that his heart is as sweet as the music he sings. With Bahá'u'lláh, on the other hand, I know that His words are only a veiled reflection of the purity and power of His soul. The only way I can stop myself from falling in love with Him is by denying myself access to His Voice.

If you want to fall in love with Bahá'u'lláh, read His Writings.

In other words, if you want to fall in love with Bahá'u'lláh, read His Writings *every day.* Simple as that.

Come on, you may think, it must be more complicated than that! Don't I have to face East or memorize something or give to the Fund or something like that? Well, yes, if you want to you can. But for me that is not the essential thing. There are, however, some ways of reading His writings that I believe are more conducive to love than others.

Reading with Love

First of all, imagine that you have just gotten a letter from your beloved. It is hand-written on scented paper. It is addressed just to you, for your eyes only. Do you:

1) Let your neighbor read it and tell you what it says?

2) Read the first sentence, memorize it, and say it once a day while throwing the rest of the letter away?

3) Get out a red pen and look for grammatical errors?

4) Analyze it for deep hidden meanings?

5) Decide that since you agree with and understand all the facts presented, you can now throw the letter away?

6) Read it over and over and over again just because it makes you smile to know you are loved?

If you answered #6, then you will probably find yourself falling in love fairly quickly if you make a commitment to read some of Bahá'u'lláh's Writings every day. The rest of you are not doing anything *wrong*. In fact there is a time and place for each of these responses. We do need to get other people's opinions now and then, memorize the obligatory prayers, think critically about what we are reading, and make sure we understand the concepts Bahá'u'lláh is presenting. But we must set aside a little bit of time each day to read *just for the love of God.* Listen to His words, and, like the words of a favorite song, let them soak in and fill your soul. Then you will truly "*soar on the wings of the Divine verses*" and thirst for spirituality.

*We must set aside a little bit of time each day to read **just for the love of God.***

PRAY

When it comes to prayer, Bahá'ís are doubly blessed. When we read the Word of God every day, our hearts are moved and we fall more deeply in love with our Creator. In this state, we will naturally wish to communicate with Him through prayer. And since Bahá'ís have hundreds of prayers which are themselves the revealed Word of God, the *reading of these prayers itself* reinforces the loving longing that they are written to express. It is a positive feedback loop that operates on so many physical, psychological and spiritual levels that it is beyond our ability to comprehend.

If one friend feels love for another, he will wish to say so. Though he knows that the friend is aware that he loves him, he will still wish to say so.... God knows the wishes of all hearts. But the impulse to prayer is a natural one, springing from man's love to God.

...Prayer need not be in words, but rather in thought and attitude. But if this love and this desire are lacking, it is useless to try to force them. Words without love mean nothing. If a person talks to you as an unpleasant duty, with no love or pleasure in his meeting with you, do you wish to converse with him?

'Abdu'l-Bahá: *Bahá'u'lláh and the New Era*, pg. 94

Know thou, verily, it is becoming in a weak one to supplicate to the Strong One, and it behooveth a seeker of bounty to beseech the Glorious Bountiful One. When one supplicates to his Lord, turns to Him and seeks bounty from His Ocean, this supplication brings light to his heart, illumination to his sight, life to his soul and exaltation to his being.

During thy supplications to God and thy reciting, "Thy Name is my healing," consider how thine heart is cheered, thy soul delighted by the spirit of the love of God, and thy mind attracted to the Kingdom of God! By these attractions one's ability and capacity increase. When the vessel is enlarged the water increases, and when the thirst grows the bounty of the cloud becomes agreeable to the taste of man. This is the mystery of supplication and the wisdom of stating one's wants.

'Abdu'l-Bahá: Bahá'u'lláh and the New Era, *Pg. 93*

Here are some new thoughts I've had about prayer:

- Prayers are not lawyers arguing a case before a skeptical Judge.
- Prayers are not letters to Santa Clause
- Prayers are not credit card applications.
- Prayers are not negotiating tools.
- Prayers are not flattery.
- Prayers don't get us somewhere, they just move us in a direction.
- Prayers don't tell God what to give us, they remind us what God has to offer.
- Prayers are not lists of what we *do* want, they attract us towards what we *should* want.
- Prayer is like touching the surface of a mirror that is turned towards the sun. Prayer is becoming the mirror.
- Prayer is like touching a cold piece of steel to a powerful magnet. Prayer is becoming magnetic.
- Prayer is like singing alone in the shower just because, because, because. Prayer is becoming the song.
- Prayer is like drinking from a cool, clear spring. Prayer is becoming pure water, returning to the sea.
- There are prayers that we say because we think they will impress or influence God or the people around us. There are prayers we say because we can't keep them from pouring out of our hearts.
- There are prayers that we memorize so that we can say them when we need to. There are prayers that inscribe themselves in fire upon our hearts.

For some of you, prayer is a very powerful experience. Perhaps you've experienced miracles as a result of specific prayers, or perhaps you feel the presence of God every time you pray. A friend of mine was hypnotized so that she feels spiritual ecstasy every time she prays.

That's great. But it is not necessary.

You don't need to worry if you've never felt that special mystical connection that other people talk about. Prayer has an effect on your soul, even *"though [you] may, at first, remain unaware of its effect."* Here's how:

The Magnetic Power of Prayer

Think of God's love as an attractive force—a magnetic force, if you will. It lends power to those things that are aligned with it and draws them to it. Now imagine your own soul like a piece of steel. A piece of steel is made up of atoms—each of which is a tiny magnet with a positive and negative pole. Likewise, every part of you—your personality and character, your thoughts and feelings—are capable of turning towards virtues and being aligned with God. In practice, however, your different parts are pointed every which-way. Money, sex, success, pleasure, food and many other distractions pull your inner qualities away from alignment with God.

The word of God, whether it is in the form of a prayer or other sacred Scripture, acts as a magnet on the cold steel of your soul.

The word of God, whether it is in the form of a prayer or other sacred Scripture, acts as a magnet on the cold steel of your soul. Have you ever touched a magnet to a nail and watched what happens? The entire nail becomes a magnet while they are in contact.

But here is the exciting part. Have you seen what the long-term effect of a powerful magnet can be on a lowly nail? Over time, the magnet permanently realigns some of the atoms of the nail so that eventually the nail itself can become a powerful magnet.

Every time we pray, we align ourselves with God. We touch the infinite and then let go. We touch the infinite and then let go. At first the effect is literally microscopic, but in time, all of those microscopic elements of our soul begin to align with the Will of God—and with each other! We become magnetic and attractive. Our virtues begin to have an influence on our surroundings. We discover that we attract the virtues and blessings of the people around us. We begin to "live the life." Though we may never have had a specific life-changing experience with prayer, we have been changed by it nevertheless.

It is interesting to note that, for steel, there are two ways to increase its power of attraction. One is to expose it to the magnet more frequently. The other is to heat it to a molten state and then let it cool in the presence of the magnet.

Likewise, if we wish to attract and be attracted to more of God's virtues, we can either increase the frequency of our casual communion with God, or we can wait until the fire of tribulation inspires us to turn to God in passionate prayer. Either will work.

Intone, O My servant, the verses of God that have been received by thee, as intoned by them who have drawn nigh unto Him, that the sweetness of thy melody may kindle thine own soul, and attract the hearts of all men. Whoso reciteth, in the privacy of his chamber, the verses revealed by God, the scattering angels of the Almighty shall scatter abroad the fragrance of the words uttered by his mouth, and shall cause the heart of every righteous man to throb. Though he may, at first, remain unaware of its effect, yet the virtue of the grace vouchsafed unto him must needs sooner or later exercise its influence upon his soul. Thus have the mysteries of the Revelation of God been decreed by virtue of the Will of Him Who is the Source of power and wisdom.

Bahá'u'lláh: Gleanings from the Writings of Bahá'u'lláh, *pg. 295*

meditate

This is the part of the process that even many long-time Bahá'ís forget. If we say our prayers and then jump up and start doing the exact same things we have always done, then how can God suggest that we do anything different? In a sense, prayer is a way for us to speak to God. It is only fair, then, that we allow an equal amount of time for listening.

Bahá'u'lláh says there is a sign (from God) in every phenomenon: the sign of the intellect is contemplation and the sign of contemplation is silence, because it is impossible for a man to do two things at one time – he cannot both speak and meditate.

It is an axiomatic fact that while you meditate you are speaking with your own spirit. In that state of mind you put certain questions to your spirit and the spirit answers: the light breaks forth and the reality is revealed....

Through the faculty of meditation man attains to eternal life; through it he receives the breath of the Holy Spirit – the bestowal of the Spirit is given in reflection and meditation.

The spirit of man is itself informed and strengthened during meditation; through it affairs of which man knew nothing are unfolded before his view. Through it he receives Divine inspiration, through it he receives heavenly food.

Meditation is the key for opening the doors of mysteries. In that state man abstracts himself: in that state man withdraws himself from all outside objects; in that subjective mood he is immersed in the ocean of spiritual life and can unfold the secrets of things-in-themselves. To illustrate this, think of man as endowed with two kinds of sight; when the power of insight is being used the outward power of vision does not see.

This faculty of meditation frees man from the animal nature, discerns the reality of things, puts man in touch with God.

This faculty brings forth from the invisible plane the sciences and arts. Through the meditative faculty inventions are made possible, colossal undertakings are carried out; through it governments can run smoothly. Through this faculty man enters into the very Kingdom of God....

The meditative faculty is akin to the mirror; if you put it before earthly objects it will reflect them. Therefore if the spirit of man is contemplating earthly subjects he will be informed of these.

But if you turn the mirror of your spirits heavenwards, the heavenly constellations and the rays of the Sun of Reality will be reflected in your hearts, and the virtues of the Kingdom will be obtained.

'Abdu'l-Bahá: Paris Talks, *pp. 174-176*

to live the life – "Be as I am."

I would like to end this book with a question for you to meditate upon: What does it mean to be a Bahá'í?

When 'Abdu'l-Bahá said "Be as I am," He did not say, "Do as I do." I personally believe that joining the Bahá'í Faith is not about *doing* the Bahá'í Faith, but about *being* a Bahá'í to the best of our ability - which in reality means *being our true selves* to the best of our ability. That is what 'Abdu'l-Bahá did. He was Himself, *and He did it perfectly.*

'Abdu'l-Bahá said "Be as I am," He did not say, "Do as I do."

Bahá'u'lláh is *not "out there,"* He is *"in here."* We see Him reflected "in here" when we turn the mirrors of our spirits to the Writings. We live the life when we *bring that reflection with us* into our interactions with the Community, the principles and the laws.

Turn thy sight unto thyself, that thou mayest find Me standing within thee, mighty, powerful and self-subsisting.

Bahá'u'lláh: The Hidden Words, *Arabic #13*

You are a Bahá'í. It is the most amazing, exciting, wondrous, awe-inspiring and profoundly humbling state of being in the universe.

Wow!!

How resplendent the luminaries of knowledge that shine in an atom, and how vast the oceans of wisdom that surge within a drop! To a supreme degree is this true of man, who, among all created things, hath been invested with the robe of such gifts, and hath been singled out for the glory of such distinction. For in him are potentially revealed all the attributes and names of God to a degree that no other created being hath excelled or surpassed. All these names and attributes are applicable to him. Even as He hath said: "Man is My mystery, and I am his mystery." Manifold are the verses that have been repeatedly revealed in all the Heavenly Books and the Holy Scriptures, expressive of this most subtle and lofty theme. Even as He hath revealed: "We will surely show them Our signs in the world and within themselves." Again He saith: "And also in your own selves: will ye not, then, behold the signs of God?" And yet again He revealeth: "And be ye not like those who forget God, and whom He hath therefore caused to forget their own selves." In this connection, He Who is the eternal King – may the souls of all that dwell within the mystic Tabernacle be a sacrifice unto Him – hath spoken: "He hath known God who hath known himself."

Bahá'u'lláh: Gleanings from the Writings of Bahá'u'lláh, *pp. 177-178*

You must thank God that your efforts are high and noble, that your endeavors are worthy, that your intentions are centered upon the Kingdom of God and that your supreme desire is the acquisition of eternal virtues. You must act in accordance with these requirements. A man may be a Bahá'í in name only. If he is a Bahá'í in reality, his deeds and actions will be decisive proofs of it. What are the requirements? Love for mankind, sincerity toward all, reflecting the oneness of the world of humanity, philanthropy, becoming enkindled with the fire of the love of God, attainment to the knowledge of God and that which is conducive to human welfare.

'Abdu'l-Bahá: The Promulgation of Universal Peace, *pg. 336*

Never speak disparagingly of others, but praise without distinction. Pollute not your tongues by speaking evil of another. Recognize your enemies as friends, and consider those who wish you evil as the wishers of good. You must not see evil as evil and then compromise with your opinion, for to treat in a smooth, kindly way one whom you consider evil or an enemy is hypocrisy, and this is not worthy or allowable. You must consider your enemies as your friends, look upon your evil-wishers as your well-wishers and treat them accordingly. Act in such a way that your heart may be free from hatred. Let not your heart be offended with anyone. If some one commits an error and wrong toward you, you must instantly forgive him. Do not complain of others. Refrain from reprimanding them, and if you wish to give admonition or advice, let it be offered in such a way that it will not burden the bearer. Turn all your thoughts toward bringing joy to hearts. Beware! Beware! lest ye offend any heart. Assist the world of humanity as much as possible. Be the source of consolation to every sad one, assist every weak one, be helpful to every indigent one, care for every sick one, be the cause of glorification to every lowly one, and shelter those who are overshadowed by fear.

In brief, let each one of you be as a lamp shining forth with the light of the virtues of the world of humanity. Be trustworthy, sincere, affectionate and replete with chastity. Be illumined, be spiritual, be divine, be glorious, be quickened of God, be a Bahá'í.

'Abdu'l-Bahá: The Promulgation of Universal Peace, *pp. 453*

Be illumined, be spiritual, be divine, be glorious, be quickened of God, be a Bahá'í.

Try with all your hearts to be willing channels for God's Bounty. For I say unto you that He has chosen you to be His messengers of love throughout the world, to be His bearers of spiritual gifts to man, to be the means of spreading unity and concord on the earth. Thank God with all your hearts that such a privilege has been given unto you. For a life devoted to praise is not too long in which to thank God for such a favor.

Lift up your hearts above the present and look with eyes of faith into the future! Today the seed is sown, the grain falls upon the earth, but behold the day will come when it shall rise a glorious tree and the branches thereof shall be laden with fruit. Rejoice and be glad that this day has dawned, try to realize its power, for it is indeed wonderful! God has crowned you with honor and in your hearts has He set a radiant star; verily the light thereof shall brighten the whole world!

'Abdu'l-Bahá: Paris Talks, pg. 68

Epilogue

As I mentioned in my introduction, much has happened in the years since I first wrote this book. I will not go into the painful details, but I would like to offer a few additional words of comfort and support for those who are struggling to remain Bahá'ís. As I have discovered, for those of us who truly love Bahá'u'lláh, the biggest tests are not with drinking, drugs, or sex–or with specific individuals in the community. We can struggle through the pain caused by our own personal tests. What is difficult is observing the pain caused by the tests of the greater Bahá'í community.

To myself and to you, I offer this simple reminder: *"For the faith of no man can be conditioned by any one except himself." Gleanings pg.145*

It was only when I gave up trying to be happy with "the Faith" or make "the Faith" happy with me that I was able to become happy with my *personal* faith. This is what has to come first. I have to find that *still quiet voice* in my heart that first lead me to Bahá'u'lláh, and then follow it no matter where it leads. If my relationship to the community hits another rough spot, it won't change a thing in my relationship with God. It is possible to remain attached to Bahá'u'lláh while temporarily detaching oneself from the Community. Indeed, statistics indicate that there are four times as many inactive Bahá'ís as active Bahá'ís in the United States. I am sure that many of them still carry the love of Bahá'u'lláh in their hearts. That's a lot of invisible lovers of God out there. If, for some reason, you or I find ourselves temporarily identified with this silent majority, then know that we are not alone, and we are not abandoned by God. God may even find ways for us to find and support one another while we–or the community–undergo transformation. You can always find me on the web.

Appendix 1

Analyzing Your Trouble Spots

Principles

The following is a list of over 80 Bahá'í principles. I invite you to seriously consider each of these principles and rate them in terms of how well you think you intellectually understand them, and then again in terms of how well you think you have really emotionally and spiritually internalized them. You get to decide what code to use. 5-1 or 1-100, X or +, Y or N, whatever works for you. This way no one else knows how you scored yourself.

You may find, for example, that you really understand the idea that God loves you, but have a difficult time feeling that love. You may find that the social teachings are easier to understand but harder to live than the metaphysical ones. Everyone is different. Being honest about where you stand will allow you to identify areas in which you need deepening and/or practice. It will also remind you of where your strengths are so that you can return to them when you lose your bearings.

This is not a test. You only fail if you fail to learn something about yourself.

Teachings about Religion:

__ __The purpose of religion is to promote love and unity between all people. A religion that promotes conflict is worse than no religion at all.

__ __There is only One God, Who loves all of humanity equally.

__ __God is a perfect *Creator,* while humanity is His perfect *creation.*

__ __In *creation*, perfection includes the capacity to grow and develop.

__ __When a human soul grows, it moves from ignorance to knowledge, from childishness to wisdom.

__ __For humans to grow in knowledge and wisdom, they need teachers.

__ __Because God loves all of humanity, He sent us many Teachers at different times and places. They are known as Messengers, Manifestations or Prophets of God.

__ __Humans (individually and collectively) are in a two-way relationship with God. God has promised to love and guide us forever. In return, we must promise to love His Messengers, and follow (or obey) Their guidance. This two-way agreement is called The Greater Covenant.

__ __God's Messengers teach us how to know, love and worship God; how to develop our virtues; and how to work together so that civilization as a whole can advance.

__ __In the past, society needed an educated clergy to pass on the teachings of the Prophet. Now that literacy is widespread, people can take responsibility for their own spiritual education.

__ __It is up to each of us to investigate the Truth and try to live in harmony with God's spiritual, moral and social teachings.

__ __Our motive for following God's teachings is *not* that we feel guilty when we *don't* follow them, but rather that we experience more joy, radiance, inner peace and closeness to God when we *do*.

Spiritual Teachings:

__ __Joy comes from knowing that we are living in harmony with our true purpose in life, which is to know and love God.

__ __The *essence* of God is not something our rational minds can comprehend, but the *qualities* of God, like generosity and mercy, are reflected in our hearts.

__ __To know God is to know His *spiritual* qualities, and to *love* God is to *love* His spiritual qualities.

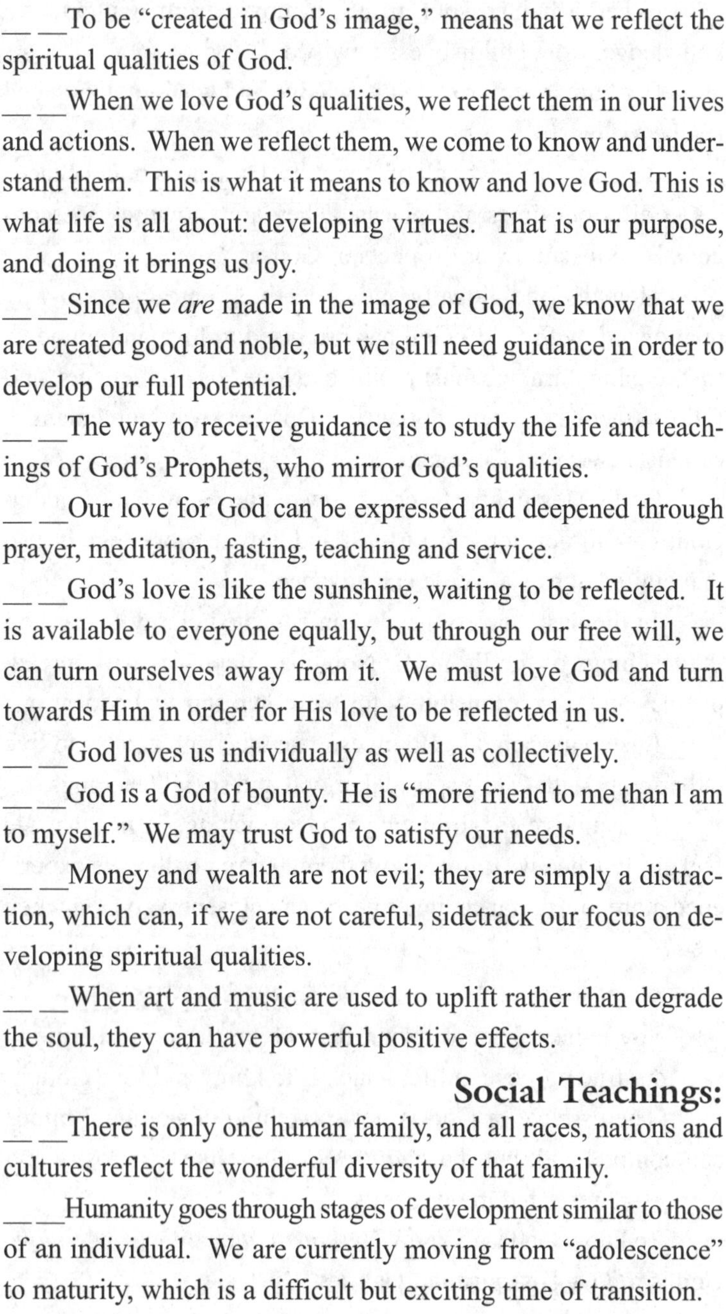

__ __To be "created in God's image," means that we reflect the spiritual qualities of God.

__ __When we love God's qualities, we reflect them in our lives and actions. When we reflect them, we come to know and understand them. This is what it means to know and love God. This is what life is all about: developing virtues. That is our purpose, and doing it brings us joy.

__ __Since we *are* made in the image of God, we know that we are created good and noble, but we still need guidance in order to develop our full potential.

__ __The way to receive guidance is to study the life and teachings of God's Prophets, who mirror God's qualities.

__ __Our love for God can be expressed and deepened through prayer, meditation, fasting, teaching and service.

__ __God's love is like the sunshine, waiting to be reflected. It is available to everyone equally, but through our free will, we can turn ourselves away from it. We must love God and turn towards Him in order for His love to be reflected in us.

__ __God loves us individually as well as collectively.

__ __God is a God of bounty. He is "more friend to me than I am to myself." We may trust God to satisfy our needs.

__ __Money and wealth are not evil; they are simply a distraction, which can, if we are not careful, sidetrack our focus on developing spiritual qualities.

__ __When art and music are used to uplift rather than degrade the soul, they can have powerful positive effects.

Social Teachings:

__ __There is only one human family, and all races, nations and cultures reflect the wonderful diversity of that family.

__ __Humanity goes through stages of development similar to those of an individual. We are currently moving from "adolescence" to maturity, which is a difficult but exciting time of transition.

__ __The transition into the global equivalent of "maturity" will involve a certain level of chaos and difficulty, but will also release wonderful new potential.

__ __Many people focus on the chaos and problems in the world and become frightened and confused, but if we look at our potential, we have reason to be optimistic. After all, we go through adolescence towards the *beginning* of our lives, not the end.

__ __World Peace is not only possible, but is the only reasonable expectation for a mature human race. A World Parliament is needed to organize and maintain global peace and cooperation.

__ __Economic and environmental problems can be solved through the application of spiritual principles.

__ __Women and men are equal in their capacity to reflect the image, or virtues of God. God is neither male nor female. The word "He" is often used in scripture only because we do not have a neutral personal pronoun in English.

__ __The family is the building block of civilization and needs to be strengthened and supported.

__ __Education of children is one of the most important forms of service possible.

__ __Science and Religion are simply two different ways of exploring God's creation and should be in harmony.

__ __The world needs an international auxiliary language to allow better communication and greater cooperation and trust between peoples. This will promote world peace.

__ __The material world is a classroom, which we should utilize, respect and preserve for future generations.

__ __While meditation and periods of solitude are valuable, we should remain active in the world and not isolate ourselves.

__ __All work done in the spirit of service is counted as worship.

Metaphysical Teachings:

__ __God is the Creator. He is not *in* His creation, nor is He *separate* from His creation. He is *reflected* in creation the way a mirror reflects the sun, or a piece of music reflects the spirit of the composer. The relationship between the Creator and creation is eternal.

__ __The rational soul is God's greatest gift to humans, but it is still limited in its ability to understand *itself,* let alone its unknowable Creator. All we can know about God are those qualities that are already reflected within us.

__ __Each of us is unique. Our uniqueness is a result of spiritual, biological and environmental factors.

__ __The soul is immortal. If it is attracted to the attributes of God, it will be strengthened and continue to move towards God after death. If not, it will weaken and fade.

__ __There is no locked door between "heaven" and "hell." Heaven is simply moving towards God. Hell is moving away. If you love truth, justice and kindness, then you will move towards God, no matter what you call yourself.

__ __For a spiritually strong person, death is the door to true life. We will retain our identities and communicate with loved ones. We will not return to the physical world. We will continue to grow and serve in the spiritual world.

__ __The soul exists independent of time and space as we know it. The soul is not "in" the body, any more than a light is "in" a mirror, or a broadcast is "in" a radio. The connection is real, but intangible.

__ __Evil is simply the absence of good in the same way as darkness is the absence of light. Though the darkness of hatred or immorality can be inconvenient, it is not a force to be fought, but rather a need to be filled by the light of love and virtue.

__ __There is a lot more to creation than we can ever imagine. The world is not an illusion, nor is it a game.

__ __We are not God, nor are we gods, nor are we Manifestations of God. But that's okay because being unique, loved, spiritual reflections of God, with the free-will capacity to love and serve, is quite enough for any soul to handle.

__ __The human soul is different from the animal spirit and reflects more of God's attributes.

__ __The human species has always been distinct, though it may have gone through evolutionary stages resembling animals.

__ __The soul or spirit of the individual comes into being with the conception of his physical body.

__ __The spiritual powers of the human soul include imagination, thought, comprehension, memory and the "common faculty" which is the interface between these inner powers and the body.

__ __When we die, we will have *spiritual* communication and vision, and move outside the realms of time or space. Trying to develop these abilities *before we die* can damage our souls and slow our progress in the afterlife.

__ __Our connection with humanity is strengthened by love of God and love for each other – not through drugs or psychic experimenting.

About God's Messengers:

__ __There are two kinds of Prophets or Teachers – Primary Messengers, like Moses, Jesus, Mohammed, Buddha and Bahá'u'lláh, and secondary messengers, like Isaiah and St. John, who received their inspiration from the others.

__ __The Primary Messengers (what Bahá'ís call "Manifestations of God"), receive their enlightenment from God and know more about creation (us) than we know about ourselves.

__ __We need these Manifestations of God in order to help us understand the difference between what is true and what we simply *wish* were true. Teachers often tell us things we would prefer not to hear or believe.

__ __All Manifestations are equal in knowledge and spirit, but the richness of their teachings was limited by their followers' abilities to understand.

__ __God's Teachers directed the progress of civilization, either directly or indirectly, and built upon each other's contributions.

__ __God's Messengers have not come to *save* us because we are inherently evil, but rather to *educate* us, because we are inherently ignorant and in need of guidance.

__ __Manifestations bring two kinds of teachings – spiritual and social. The spiritual teachings are eternal, but the social teachings change to meet the needs of the time.

__ __The Prophets spoke in parables and symbols, and those who have "eyes to see and ears to hear" read scripture from that perspective.

__ __The Manifestations of God are perfect *reflections* of God, they are not God in His Essence, nor are they little *pieces* of God.

__ __God, His Messengers and the Holy Spirit are what Christians call The Father, The Christ and The Holy Ghost. These three can be likened to the sun, a perfect mirror and the light that reflects off the mirror to create a perfect image of the Sun. While the sun never leaves the sky, the mirror (Messenger) can still be said to represent the sun (God) on earth through the power of its light (Holy Spirit).

__ __Jesus was born of a virgin and was the *spiritual* Son, not the physical Son of God. God's spiritual "Son" rose *spiritually* to a spiritual Heaven to live forever.

__ __The term "return" refers to a return of the spiritual qualities or spiritual station of Prophets, not their physical return. For example, Jesus said that John the Baptist was the return of Elias, even though physically, John was His cousin.

__ __One can tell a true Prophet from a false one by the "fruit" of His teachings and the example of His life.

Administrative Principles:

__ __Administrative bodies are elected by secret ballot with no campaigning and no nominations. In a tie between a member of a minority and someone else, the minority representative fills the position.

__ __Decisions are made through consultation. In consultation, ideas do not "belong" to any individual, but rather to the group. Don't be stubborn or mean. Don't whine and don't be manipulative with your words or emotions.

__ __Steps in consultation are: Determining the facts, determining the principles involved, discussing options, making sure everyone has been heard from, arriving at consensus or taking a vote and then universally and wholeheartedly supporting the decision.

__ __There are no "no" votes, only "yes" votes and abstentions. If the majority do not vote *for* a proposal, then it fails. You only need a majority of those present, not all members (provided there is at least a quorum present).

__ __The Assembly answers to God, not the Community. If members of the Community disagree, they can appeal or ask the Assembly to reconsider, but they can't try to pressure or "outvote" the Assembly.

__ __In any consultation, the body is free to make different decisions under seemingly identical situations, as long as law and principle are both upheld.

Moral Teachings:

__ __Everything in God's Creation is connected in some way. All human souls are connected spiritually, which means that we affect and influence one another in ways we don't always realize. The good or harm we do unto others also affects us.

__ __When we remember that we are primarily *spiritual* beings, and also recognize the fact that we are *spiritually connected* to everyone else on earth, then most moral and ethical teachings become easier to understand.

__ __We should strive to strengthen our spiritual capacities, which include: generosity, kindness, patience, forgiveness, cleanliness, chastity, honesty and trustworthiness, justice, wisdom, intellectual perception, equity, truthfulness, benevolence, courage, fortitude, respect, rectitude, self-sacrifice, obedience, service to God and guidance and education of others. This is just a starting point.

__ __"The Golden Rule" is a natural expression of our sense of connection to everyone else – even those people who *seem* like they are our enemies.

__ __We should work on our own faults, ignore others' faults and avoid "backbiting."

__ __Parents should love and educate their children. Children should honor and serve their parents.

__ __Some people are motivated by reward, others by punishment. Most of us require both, so God's Justice includes both. Punishment is *not* the same as vengeance.

__ __When sick, we should use *both* prayer and the best medical advice available.

Analyzing Our Trouble Spots

Laws

If you've made it this far, I guess you are ready to take a look at your relationship to Bahá'í Laws. This list was not meant to be your first introduction to Bahá'í Law. I assume that you have read one of the other introductory "Welcome to the Community" books that explains the Bahá'í Laws in greater detail before you got here.

This list has an entirely different purpose. Here, I encourage you to consider the degree to which you feel you understand the spiritual logic behind a law, and then the ease with which you think you will be able to obey it. This will help you become aware of potential problems, especially around laws that you don't understand, that you are likely to break and which carry sanctions. If you find several, then please go find someone you trust and ask for support. Look for the attribute of God that the law is designed to develop, and try to love it. Also pray for strength and understanding. But also give yourself credit for all of the many laws that you find easy to obey.

Personal Laws Between You and God

All laws become binding at the age of 15

__ __Read the Sacred Writings every morning and evening

__ __Say one of the three obligatory prayers every day

__ __And follow the directions that go with them

__ __Say Alláh'u'Abhá 95 times every day

__ __Practice consultation when making decisions

__ __Engage in an occupation that both supports you financially and is of service to humanity

__ __Avoid idleness and sloth and do not beg

__ __Educate your children, especially your girl children

__ __Keep yourself, your clothes and your home clean

__ __Go on pilgrimage if at all possible

Social Laws between You and God

__ __Teach other people about the Faith.

Participate in Bahá'í Community life, including:

__ __Attend Feast

__ __Contribute to the Fund

__ __Pay Huqúqu'lláh

__ __Participate in Bahá'í elections

__ __Observe Holy Days

__ __Observe the 19 Day Fast

__ __Write a Will and have a Bahá'í burial

__ __Be buried, not cremated

__ __Lead a chaste life, with all of its many implications

__ __Avoid cruelty to animals

__ __Avoid partisan politics and conflicts

__ __Avoid carrying weapons unless absolutely necessary

Laws For Which There Are Sanctions

Certain behaviors have such a strong impact on you and society at large that the Bahá'í Administration is authorized to exert direct pressure upon individuals to encourage obedience. These include:

__ __Gossip that undermines the unity of the Community

__ __Flagrant use of alcoholic beverages

__ __Use of narcotic drugs unless prescribed by a doctor

__ __Gambling

__ __Flagrant sexual activity outside of marriage

__ __Flagrant homosexual activity

__ __Joining a political party or running for political office

__ __Violating civil law

Violating Bahá'í marriage laws. *These include requirements to:*

__ __Get consent from all living parents

__ __Say the vow *"We will all, verily, abide by the Will of God"*

__ __Have Assembly approval of two witnesses

__ __Go through a "year of waiting" before getting divorced

We are to remain loyal and obedient to our government unless to do so would require us to break another Bahá'í law. Many civil laws parallel Bahá'í laws, including those against:

__ __murder

__ __arson

__ __theft

__ __battery

__ __trespassing

Other Laws

These are laws which are not yet binding on non-Persians, or that probably do not apply to your daily life

__ __Husband's payment of a dowry to his wife

__ __Various laws on inheritance

Prohibitions against:

__ __Multiple spouses

__ __Slave trading

__ __Asceticism and monasticism (being a Monk)

__ __Priesthood, pulpits and kissing of hands

__ __The sacrament of Confession *(not to be confused with* simply talking with friends about mistakes you've made).

__ __Saying your daily obligatory prayer as a group

__ __Muttering Sacred Writings in public to appear holy

__ __Plunging your hand into public sources of food

__ __Shaving your head

Appendix 2

Especially Troubling Laws

There are two Bahá'í laws that many politically progressive Bahá'ís find particularly troubling. When I became a Bahá'í in the early 1970's, they were not "hot buttons," because people had different ideas of what was politically and morally correct. Now, they are often the first issues to come up when discussing the Faith with "liberal" seekers and new Bahá'ís.

I was encouraged to leave these questions out of a book for new Bahá'ís. I was told they are too controversial. They will distract people from the other issues. They are better left for later. But as a new Bahá'í, these issues could be among the very first your friends ask you about. You can't put their questions on hold, and you can't put your own mind on hold either.

Women on the Universal House of Justice

At my first meeting with a very intelligent and politically active woman, I told her I was a member of the Bahá'í Faith. Her very first question was, "In your religion, are there women at the highest level of the governing hierarchy?"

I was stunned. I didn't get to tell her about progressive revelation. I didn't get to warm her up with race unity and the equality of women and men. All I could do was smile and say, "It is fascinating that you would ask that particular question." But the smile was forced, and the conversation quickly took a downward turn.

I knew at that moment that I needed to become comfortable with this issue. There is no way to avoid it, and if my response is evasive, apologetic or resistant, then people will justifiably tune me out.

I have since come up with a response to that question. I will share it with you, and then try to explain why and how I decided on it. I am not claiming that it is the best, most correct or most popular response, and I am not asking you to accept it as your own. I am simply offering it to those of you who are dissatisfied with the other answers floating around out there.

> Are there women on the Universal House of Justice? No. There are not. The Bahá'í Faith does not claim to be a Utopia. If it did, you would be right to reject it. It only claims to be the best system that humanity as a whole will be willing and able to implement within the next 900 years. At this point, we are working very hard just to promote the equality of women and men. It isn't easy - not in India, not in Africa and not in the United States. (Surely you have noticed that even in the US, they have not passed the Equal Rights Amendment.) But by the time the next Messenger comes, one of two things will have happened. Either all of humanity will have been prepared to have women on the Universal House of Justice, or everyone will be completely aware of the reasons why they will not be.

This explanation is an extension of the idea I presented in the section on law—that there is a difference between the ideal and the pragmatic. Ideal law would forbid smoking, make us all vegetarians, and demonstrate equality in every single aspect of human endeavor. But pragmatic law—the law of wisdom—only asks of us what we are willing and able to accept within a reasonable amount of time, with a reasonable amount of education, guidance and prodding.

'Abdu'l-Bahá did not say that the *reason* for the law would become clear as the noonday sun. He said that the *wisdom* of the law would become clear. Wisdom reminds us that there is a difference between a spiritual principle and the best path for manifesting that principle in the world. It is like the difference between giving directions to Haifa "as the eagle flies" and "as the human walks."

The House of Justice, however, according to the explicit text of the Law of God, is confined to men; this for a wisdom of the Lord God's, which will ere long be made manifest as clearly as the sun at high noon.

'Abdu'l-Bahá: Selections from the Writings of 'Abdu'l-Bahá, *pg. 80*

In Western countries, there are many women who are understandably hurt and confused by this law. But around the world (and even in those same countries), there may be many many more men and women who would simply not be able to accept the authority of the Universal House of Justice if it included women. They may not be ready for 100% of this truth, just as we "liberal thinkers" may not be ready for 100% of some other spiritual truth. The good of the whole requires a balance that maintains the strength of the Covenant. Are we strong enough to adjust our hopes and needs to accommodate the capacity of the rest of the world? Do we really think we would achieve equality faster *without* Bahá'u'lláh's help?

The following quotation clearly relates the idea of wisdom to tact and patience rather than innate spiritual differences between men and women, and 'Abdu'l-Bahá was clearly exercising this tact *within* the Community.

I am endeavouring, with Bahá'u'lláh's confirmations and assistance, so to improve the world of the handmaidens that all will be astonished. This progress is intended to be in spirituality, in virtues, in human perfections and in divine knowledge. In America, the cradle of women's liberation, women are still debarred from political institutions because they squabble. They are yet to have a member in the House of Representatives. Also Bahá'u'lláh hath proclaimed: "O ye men of the House of Justice." Ye need to be calm and composed, so that the work will proceed with wisdom, otherwise there will be such chaos that ye will leave everything and run away. "This newly born babe is traversing in one night the path that needeth a hundred years to tread." In brief, ye should now engage in matters of pure spirituality and not contend with men. 'Abdu'l-Bahá will tactfully take appropriate steps. Be assured. In the end thou wilt thyself exclaim, "This was indeed supreme wisdom!" I appeal to you to obliterate this contention between men and women....

No one can on his own achieve anything. 'Abdu'l-Bahá must be well pleased and assist.

'Abdu'l-Bahá: Women, *(A Compilation), Selection #11*

The idea that the Bahá'ís themselves would reject a House of Justice with female members is only a theory, but it is based on some interesting facts. For example, the incidents of domestic violence increase in some countries when women become more educated and active in their communities. In many countries, female pioneers are elected to offices, but local women are still left off of Assemblies. Even in Iran, Shoghi Effendi had to force the Bahá'ís to elect a woman to the National Spiritual Assembly. But it is not just developing countries that have difficulties accepting women in power. In the US, "cradle of liberation" that we are, we still haven't passed the Equal Rights Amendment, and there is only a handful of women in Congress.

Faced with this information, we have to ask ourselves if the cause of equality would be helped or hurt if obedience to the Universal House of Justice were undermined. If strengthening the Covenant supports the cause of women in the long run, then it really is the shortest path to equality.

In choosing this response to this issue, I considered many other theories that come up in Community discussions. At the risk of angering people, I would like to briefly mention some of the other ideas in circulation. There are theories that weaken the Covenant by suggesting that 'Abdu'l-Bahá and/or Shoghi Effendi were simply wrong. But that is inconsistent with my understanding of their stations.

There are theories that assume gender distinctions that are not supported by the Writings. Men are not from Mars. Women are not from Venus. We are both created in the image of God. So it is hard to justify theories that say that women are too merciful, sensitive, or loving to serve, or that they are not intelligent, forceful or focused enough.

> *When humanity has accepted equality, then God will show us more ways to demonstrate it.*

On the other hand, another theory is that women are *so much smarter* than men that they would speed the establishment of the New World Order along faster than the men of the world could handle. But this only turns the insult back on men, and is equally unjustified.

There are theories that patronize women by saying that they are "exempted" from serving so they can raise children. The corollary to those theories would leave men "exempted" from child rearing, and that doesn't seem right either.

There is only one other theory that I have heard that doesn't insult, patronize, or assert unfounded distinctions between men and women, but it has a different problem. As a Science Fiction fan, I have to wonder what the effect would be if a pregnant woman spent six days a week for nine months being a channel for the Holy Spirit. Would there be a risk that the baby would become more spiritually or psychically sensitive than the world is ready for? What a thought! But it is not the kind of theory you offer an atheist feminist and expect them to say, "Oh, of course, the pre-natal hyper-spiritual stimulation theory - that explains everything!"

So instead, I offer the foundation of progressive revelation–that God does not teach us what is true, He teaches us what we are able to understand as true. When humanity has accepted equality, then God will show us more ways to demonstrate it.

Addendum:

In the years since the first edition of this book, this issue has generated a great deal more heat, but little more light. Back then I said that there was no way to change this law. Now I am not so rigid in my views, and I'd like to tell you why.

I believe that the Bahá'í Community should allow those for whom it is important, to hold out the hope that the law might one day change.

First, a while back I attended a Bahá'í men's retreat with a group of really wonderful men. Somehow or other the issue of women on the House of Justice came up, and all of these men started complaining about how the women were always bellyaching over this one tiny, insignificant issue. Not one of them seemed to have an ounce of compassion for how it might feel from the other side. Finally, I turned to a young African American man and asked him how he would feel if Bahá'u'lláh had said that all of mankind was one, but no blacks could serve on the House of Justice. His eyes got wide, and he literally fell back in his chair with a look of panic and said "wow! I never thought of it like that before. You're right. I'd be really angry."

That there are any women in the Faith *at all* is a testament to their maturity and detachment, and the sooner men develop some compassion and appreciation for how it would feel to be on the other side of the issue, the sooner the community can begin to heal.

Because this is an emotional issue, not an intellectual or even theological issue, I believe that the Bahá'í Community should allow those for whom it is important, to hold out the hope that the law might one day change. It doesn't have to make sense. It doesn't have to be logical. It doesn't need to be proven one way or the other. If we simply allow for the possibility that one day someone will find a hidden tablet stuck in a crack in the plaster of some early Bahá'í's home that says there can be women on the House, then it will ease a great deal of pain.

The secondary advantage of this openness is that it will allow back into the Faith the many people who feel left out or shoved out of the Faith because they have an unorthodox opinion of this issue.

We have to accept the fact that no one knows what the future of the Faith will look like. We only know what it looks like now. As long as people are willing to live with what it is now, then their opinions about the future are irrelevant. With a hundred billion ways of understanding every quotation, surely there is room in the Faith to allow for possibilities that are outside of the mainstream. Just because I can allow for other interpretations doesn't mean I have to believe them, and just because someone else believes them doesn't mean anyone else has to agree that they are right!

This openness will allow back into the Faith the many people who feel left out or shoved out of the Faith because they have an unorthodox opinion of this issue.

When men own the equality of women there will be no need for them to struggle for their rights!

('Abdu'l-Bahá, Paris Talks, p. 163)

Homosexuality - Unhealthy, Not Evil

Many people believe that God made up a bunch of laws just to see if we were willing to follow them. There are those who say, "Yes I will" and those who say, "No I won't." There are very few who say, "God, please help me see how this law will help me become more happy and healthy."

This is why you will notice that the political debate about homosexuality avoids the obvious question of, "Is this lifestyle healthy?" and instead focuses on, "Is this evil or is this natural?" Both of *these* questions are irrelevant. "Evil" implies negative intent, and most homosexuals do not *intend* to do themselves or anyone else harm. "Natural" implies benign, but cancer, depression and alcoholism are *natural* responses to environmental stresses, and are not healthy.

Bahá'u'lláh knows better than we do what it takes to be spiritually and physically happy and healthy.

Simply put, Bahá'u'lláh knows better than we do what it takes to be spiritually and physically happy and healthy. Homosexual behavior does not lead to individual or social wellbeing.

When we are dealing with non-Bahá'ís, we must hold on to this simple truth, and not allow ourselves to get pulled into the polarizing arguments of an immature world. As I discussed in the section on shame, the rest of the world sees things in black and white. The religious right proclaims that homosexuals are "evil" and deserving of our persecution, so the rest of the country is forced into a reactive position of support. Anyone who refuses to agree that homosexuality is *good* is automatically labeled as an intolerant, hateful member of the religious right. Bahá'ís, as usual, get caught in the middle–teaching tolerance, but trying to promote healthy choices.

When talking with Bahá'ís who are struggling with homosexuality themselves, we have no choice but to love them and to try to demonstrate a healthy, moderate, mature lifestyle that manifests God's grace. Homosexual Bahá'ís are assured that it is possible to overcome this difficulty, while heterosexual Bahá'ís are reminded that this is a heavy burden not so terribly different from those we all carry.

No matter how devoted and fine the love may be between people of the same sex, to let it find expression in sexual acts is wrong. To say that it is ideal is no excuse. Immorality of every sort is really forbidden by Bahá'u'lláh, and homosexual relationships He looks upon as such, besides being against nature.

To be afflicted this way is a great burden to a conscientious soul. But through the advice and help of doctors, through a strong and determined effort, and through prayer, a soul can overcome this handicap.

God judges each soul on its own merits. The Guardian cannot tell you what the attitude of God would be towards a person who lives a good life in most ways, but not in this way. All he can tell you is that it is forbidden by Bahá'u'lláh, and that one so afflicted should struggle and struggle again to overcome it. We must be hopeful of God's Mercy but not impose upon it.

From a letter written on behalf of Shoghi Effendi, March 26,1950

Both homosexuals and heterosexuals live in a culture that defines people sexually

To regard homosexuals with prejudice and disdain would be entirely against the spirit of the Bahá'í Teachings.

Universal House of Justice, From a letter to the NSA of the US, September 11,1995

Both homosexuals and heterosexuals live in a culture that defines people sexually, glorifies sensation over relation, seeks relationships based on intensity rather than intimacy, and confuses love and lust. We must have compassion for one another's failures and celebrate each other's successes. We have much to learn from one another.

In many ways, the issue of homosexuality is a good place to end this book, because it taps into many of the issues that were presented earlier. If I were to write an in-depth discussion of homosexuality, it would explore the same issues of forgiveness, grace, tolerance, dealing with shame, understanding unconscious elements of relationships, love and intimacy, obedience, and complete trust in Bahá'u'lláh that I have already presented.

Dealing with homosexuality is no different from any other Bahá'í standard, but it can be more difficult for homosexuals to hide their struggle with Bahá'í law. It is all the more important, then, that they be made to feel just as welcome and just as *loved*, as those of us who struggle privately. When we are successful in doing this—as individuals and as a community—then we will finally understand the value of *falling into grace.* In recognizing our common struggle and forgiving ourselves our failures, we open ourselves up to intimacy. This intimacy is the only path to the loving Community that we all long for.

We really are all in this together.

Unless and until the believers really come to realize they are one spiritual family, knit together by a bond more lasting than mere physical ties can ever be, they will not be able to create that warm community atmosphere which alone can attract the hearts of humanity, frozen for lack of real love and feeling.

Shoghi Effendi 5/5/43: Guidelines for Teaching, p 312

This love amongst the believers is the magnet which will, above all else, attract the hearts and bring new souls into the Cause. Because obviously the teachings—however wonderful—cannot change the world unless the Spirit of Bahá'u'lláh's love is mirrored in the Bahá'í Communities.

On behalf of Shoghi Effendi 10/27/44: Compilation of Compilations II p. 13

Other Literature by Justice St Rain:

books:

Why Me? *A Spiritual Guide to Growing Through Tests*
My Bahá'í Faith—*A Personal Tour of the Bahá'í Teachings*

booklets:

The Secret of Happiness
One Light—Many Lamps
Poor in All Save God—A Spiritual Guide to Wealth
A Spiritual Guide to Great Sex (about chastity)
Finding Common Ground
Bahá'í Teachings for a New Millennium (*with Karen St Rain*)

pamphlets:

Nine Reasons Why You Will Want to Join the Bahá'ís
Nine Reasons to Work for Race Unity
Nine Thing Men Gain by Promoting the Equality of Women
The Power of Prayer
The Rumor of Christ's Return
Three Tools for Healing
The Gardener and the Rose

These and many other items are available online at:

www.BahaiResources.com

or call **1-800-326-1197**